REMODELING YOUR HOUSE

WITHOUT

KILLING YOUR SPOUSE

Leslie Hart-Davidson

Hart-Davidson Books
559 E. Sherwood Road
Williamston, MI 48895
www.hddbook.com

Orders by U.S. trade bookstores and wholesalers.
Please contact Distribution: Tel: (517) 889-5071 or visit www.hddbook.com.

Printed in the United States of America

First Printing, 2014

ISBN 978-0991636006

No unicorns were harmed in the making of this book. Some names and identifying details have been changed to protect the privacy of individuals.

Cover Design & Illustration Copyright © 2014 by Linda Hamlin
Book design and production by Sara Reedy
Interior illustrations © 2014 Molly Gates
Author photograph by Jill Lenkowski

with & for

Nothing in life is ever done alone. I have a tremendous amount of appreciation and love for the following folks who made this book possible. I'm fully aware of what a high-maintenance, pain-in-the-ass, procrastinating asshole I can be, so I thank you from the bottom of my heart for putting up with me as Remodeling Your House without Killing Your Spouse came to life.

To my daughter Lillian: thank you for understanding every time I replied "mama's gotta write" when you asked me to hang out. I owe you a bajillion mama/daughter mani pedis to make up for the lost time. Wait—not a bajillion. Don't hold me to that. How about 3? No? Okay, we'll negotiate later, kid.

To my husband BHD: when I sat crying in my studio the day that two crazy clients boiled over and tested my faith in design, you looked at me and told me to suck it up and just write the damn book. Thank you for making me get off my ass and finally do it. Thank you for making me start the business. Thank you for making me believe I could be a leader. Thank you for relentlessly pursuing me when I was a teenager and convincing me we could do great things together. Love!

To JenHen: taking shit-tons of time away from the studio to write this beast wouldn't have been possible without you holding down the fort and doing that awesome thing where you take care of everything in my life. Now I've had the time of my life, and I've never felt this way before. I swear, JJ, it's the truth, and I owe it all to you. Oh, and the rules of the road apply in the cracker aisle, bitch. Woof.

To the 25 generations Hart-Davidson Designs Interns: I am humbled and honored by your ridiculous talents and willingness to embrace democratic design. I'm even happier when you constantly ask "why" and push to change the current policies to better serve our clients. Special thanks to Katie Miller ('07), my very first MSU intern, for setting the bar high for all students that came after you. You rock, Katie.

To my favorite Spice girl: without your brilliance during the writing retreat weekends at Casa Cohassett, this book would still be languishing in my brain instead of released into the wild. Your love, ridonkulous cooking skills, impressive wine collection and decades of friendship made all the difference. I love you to bits, dearie. Now let's fly to Kauai for some quality drinking time & yoga on the lanai.

To my Kitten: nobody on earth has the patience and ability you possess to make me get shit done. This book simply would not exist without your awesomeness, so thank you for forcing me in that sweet way of yours to finish the book 9 minutes at a time. You constantly amaze me with your dedication and wicked talents. When I grow up, I want to be you. PURRRRRRRRRRRRRRRRRRRRRRRRRRRRRRRRRRRRRRRRRRRRRP.

To my parents: you were both always my biggest fans, so I'm sure you're cheering me on from heaven. I'm grateful for every lesson, whether intended or implied, that allowed me to gain practical skills for work and friendship and service to others. The most valuable thing I learned from you both was that kind intentions and a sense of humor can get you everywhere in life. I'm doing my level best to pass that along to my kid.

table of contents

It will all be fine in the end.
If it's not fine, it's not the end.

110
c.r.a.p

Dr. Gregory House
helps you diagnose
and treat dysfunction-
al spaces! **pg 140**

156
character

Take the Fire Test to
see how meaningful
your decor is! **pg 160**

My name is Leslie Hart-Davidson, and I'm a bacon-haired designer with an unwaivering mission to help people live better in their homes. After receiving my B.A. in Interior Design from Bowling Green State University in 1994, I spent a decade in the industry before fully launching my own design business, Hart-Davidson Designs (HDD). Despite all my extensive training, I've actually been designing since abouuuuuuut.....birth. My parents were real estate flippers in the 1970's and 80's, so I've always been in and around the world of home improvement. I'm also a fifth generation seamstress and the granddaughter of an artist who made upcycling and dumpster diving hella-cool in the 1930's. My people had one critical thing in common: they all valued knowledge and resourcefulness when it came to homes.

I was driven to pursue residential interior design as a career from the moment my mama handed me a bucket of wallpaper paste with the expectation that I help her and learn the process. I was four years old. One of my first vivid memories is the smell of the paint & wallpaper store in Springfield, Ohio where we spent hours making selections for the homes she and dad were flipping. I recall purchasing a roll of wallpaper with large-scale drawings of vintage automobiles and watching carefully as she installed it in the giant first floor closet of a project home. The process was like church for me: there was a reverence and respect for the procedure that she carried out with each measured line, each cut, each brush stroke of the paste. I watched and helped for hours, asking her questions along the way. What I learned that day with that particular pattern of wallpaper shaped the rest of my life. "Mama, why are you spending so much time on a closet?" I asked. She put down her smoothing brush, standing back and evaluating her work. "Details, LC" she replied. "Life is in the details. When potential buyers who have seen many homes in one day walk through, they'll forget the carpet and the layout, but they'll remember the details like cool wallpaper in a closet."

From that moment, I developed a different relationship with homes. I constantly searched for details and coolness in all the spaces I visited, happily sharing ideas with my mama each time I discovered something new. She was thrilled when it came time for college and I chose the interior design program at Bowling Green State University in Ohio. Through all my class projects, I offered up a level of detail that felt like second nature to me. I put as much energy and love into each assignment as I saw my mama put into each flipped house, and the effort was rewarded by my instructors. "You just get it," one practicing adjunct professor told me. When I graduated, mama gave me a beautiful watch and a note that said simply "We did it."

Today, I treat the homes of my design clients with the same energy and love that I learned from my mama at age four. Over a decade in business has taught me much about the expectations that folks have for their homes. As instrumental as mama was to my perspective on cool details in a home, my dad was just as critical in developing my people skills necessary to help clients live better in their homes.

Dad was a very social creature and was quick to read people and adjust his body language and tone to make them feel more comfortable. He would tell me stories of his married real estate clients who would fight with each other in front of him about elements of the houses they were touring. Since arguing clients meant no purchase contract (which meant no paycheck for him), dad was quick to assess the root of their argument and intervene with knowledge to help stop the fighting and guide them toward a compromise and eventual purchase. I learned much from the stories he told and realized early in my career that fears about the home—what it represents, what it can and can't do—often manifest during consultations with clients. I conjure my dad every time I break up a fight by offering a smile, a joke and some knowledge to put them back on track.

Knowledge is power. I wrote Remodeling Your House without Killing Your Spouse not only to help folks live better in their homes through edutaining lessons, but also to honor the legacy of my parents and my ancestors who all thought that homes were pretty cool.

One last thought: while I talk a good show about legacies and honor, you should know that my mama was a die-hard South Park fan and that my dad told the raunchiest jokes ever. A sense of humor, full command of popular culture and thick skin were all required for the Hart family. In

Remodeling Your House without Killing Your Spouse, you'll find ridiculous esoteric pop culture references along with plenty of foul language and comical drawings sprinkled throughout the book. If you are easily offended, put this book down and walk away now (but know that my mama will believe you to have a stick up your ass). Enjoy!

Legend of the Icons

 Insider tips from professional interior designer Leslie Hart-Davidson

 The binder in which all the worksheets and important documents live

 Warnings to avoid conflict, divorce, and homicide during your remodel

 Assignments to complete with your spouse and place in the brain binder

 Readiness to move on to the next section after assignments are completed

Democratic Design

Welcome to Remodeling Your House without Killing Your Spouse! Before we begin, I want to give you a heads up about using RYH-WKYS: this is NOT a book of room porn with glossy pictures that you'll covet and never be able to emulate in your own home. This is NOT a textbook that is so dry you'll fall asleep while reading. This is a workbook. You and your partner will need to fully participate in activities and worksheets in order to get the most out of this book and prevent homicide or divorce during your home improvement project. Keep in mind, though, that if you're unwilling to do the quick activities listed in this book and proactively plan for the project before ripping apart your home and spending gobs of cash to remodel, well.....I wouldn't have taken you on as a client because you just violated the idea of democratic design.

I genuinely wanted to help clients live better in their homes.

So what is Democratic Design? When introducing this concept to folks, I often start by telling them what it is NOT. Democratic Design isn't a political stance (though a landlord once forbade me to put that slogan on the building sign for fear of polarizing patrons). It isn't just a catchy tagline that I dreamed up one day during a marketing meeting. It is the entire way I operate my company HDD from building relationships with clients and vendors to hiring staff to mentoring 25+ generations of bright college interns. It is the very thing that defines who we are as a company and how we treat others. Democratic Design is the philosophy of "with and for", not "to and at". The principle asserts that everyone's opinion matters, and that the best design is created by listening and collaborating.

So where did the idea originate? Not me. When I discovered the idea of democratic design in 2002, it was from the perspective of how a designer should engage and relate to the client. When I first met the couple who would ultimately define my business mantra, I knew that I was both a good listener and a good designer. I genuinely wanted to help clients live better in their homes. I arrived at the consultation with the Defining Couple and was greeted warmly. The wife took my coat and whisked it away to a closet in the other room. The husband pulled me aside quickly, looked me square in the eyes and said this: "You aren't going to make my wife cry, are you?" I was stunned by his question, so I smiled back confidently and said "No sir, I wasn't planning on it." "Oh good," he said. "The last designer we had in here waltzed in like he owned the place and started pointing at all my wife's things and yelled 'That's UGLY. That's HIDEOUS! UGH! BURN THIS or I'm NOT working with you!!!' You can imagine that my wife was pretty up-

> *"Spouse" is a relative term and should be interpreted as any type of partner: domestic, parental, feline or other. Honestly, I chose the term because it rhymed with "house" for the title.*

set, especially since all the stuff he pointed at was what she just inherited from her deceased mother a few months ago."

At that precise moment, something clicked. I understood that to be a good designer and truly help clients live better in their homes, I had to look at possessions and client relationships (with me and with each other) with the same thought: tangible possessions hold weight, and words weigh heavy in the minds of clients. Balance the two and give sage advice based on good design principles, and you'll have a winning design.

> **Thing [thing], noun**
> An idea, item or element that you deem to have value, merit or coolness that "will be allowed" in your world.

After that meeting, I did a bit of research and discovered that the other prominent designers in my community practiced Dictatorial design (just like the "burn your mother's stuff" jerk). What's worse, the clientele they served actually expected that brand of service. It took several years for me to train my clients that they had a voice when it came to their décor and decisions. In fact, I vividly recall one client who had left the jerk designer saying this to me when I asked her which sink she preferred for her bathroom remodel: "Wait....you mean.....I get to choose? But....you're the designer. Isn't it up to you?" "No," I replied. "I narrowed it down for you, but you have to live with this. The choice is yours." It completely threw her that she had the power to choose. Once she made the decision, she was quiet for a minute. "You're not like the others, are you?" she asked. "No ma'am" I said. "Democracy is a THING."

I'm a fan of democracy in many aspects, but seeing spouses and families practice democratic design during a project is my favorite part of the concept. This is how Remodeling Your House without Killing Your Spouse came to be a THING: by watching the manner in which so many of my clients interacted with each other during the stress-inducing planning and execution of both small and large scale remodels. I originally wrote a seminar based on my observations of these interactions with the RYHWKYS title in 2007 for a Women's Series at Michigan State University. I had discovered during those years of spousal interactions that there were four key indicators for success in those remodels (success being defined as project completed with zero hospitalizations or divorce proceedings). The indicators were **communication, cash, CRAP,** and **character**.

The purpose of the RYHWKYS seminar was to teach those success indicators to my clients and the community at large. This book follows the same content that I've been successfully teaching for 7+ years and is filled with activities and worksheets to make the most of proactive planning and execution of your project. Specifically, I'll introduce the idea of **communication** by telling the story of Barry

Domestic Violence is NEVER a thing. The title of this book is intended to be tongue-in-cheek. If you are experiencing any type of abuse, speak up and get help.

and Carrie, whose antics will play a recurring role in this book. Second, I'll explain the pivotal role of **cash** and how money is a game-changing element of preparing and hiring the right team for your project. Next, I'll enlighten you with **CRAP**, a design language that is an acronym for **C**ontrast, **R**epetition, **A**lignment and **P**roximity. This common design language will help you to define your desires and dislikes of a space and better articulate them to your spouse and family. Finally, I'll introduce you to **character**, which boils down the importance of décor and aesthetics to defining three key elements: who you are, where you come from, and what you believe in.

A note about using RYHWKYS: Please remember that this isn't a pretty book about interior design that you peruse and troll for ideas, then forget about like last summer's book club pick. Using this book requires an investment in learning how to make your space function and feel better with the help of your partner by completing worksheets and exercises to reveal the true needs of your remodel. I'll do my very best to make the process as entertaining and educational as possible, but it's up to you to actually do the work required to be successful. Remodeling Your House without

Dic•tat•ing de•sign•er
[dik-teyt-ing] [dih-zahy-ner], noun
Traditional interior designers who closely hold all knowledge and design secrets without educating their clients during the process, then dictate the aesthetics and function of a client's space for purposes of portfolio building and trend promotion rather than helping those clients live better in their homes.

Killing Your Spouse is the equivalent of an individualized nutritional plan combined with a top-of-the-line elliptical machine: I can give you the tools to succeed, but it's up to you to decide whether to use them or sit on the couch and stuff the metaphorical box of Twinkies in your mouth.

So how do you know if you're ready to use this book? This Foxworthian list might help:

• If you've ever rolled your eyes at your spouse while in the aisle of a big box store, you might need RYHWKYS

• If you contemplated homicide while selecting paint colors, you might need RYHWKYS

• If you openly argue about remodel projects in front of your contractor or other design professional, you might need RYHWKYS

• If you already have a space in your home where you've banished your spouse because you don't want to see their stuff, you might need RYHWKYS

• If you want a successful remodel project with excellent content, a fabulous road map and a bit of humor thrown in for good measure, you might need RYHWKYS

communication

do

> **"It doesn't make for a happy life when you have a fabulous new space, but the cost was learning that your spouse is an asshole."**

learn

enjoy

The Story of Barry & Carrie

Generally, getting people to talk during a design consultation is pretty easy. Getting people to accurately express their needs for a living space is a whole different ballgame. I learned just how complicated this process could be when I met a couple who had remarkably different communication styles. Barry and Carrie sought me out to complete a remodel of their second floor living area. They had one request: "Make our out-of-state friends want to come and stay for a week to go skiing."

Their existing second floor layout was not conducive to the type of enticement they were after; the choppy rooms and tiny single bathroom smacked more of Motel 6 than a friendly week-long retreat. After measuring the space and interviewing Barry and Carrie about their specific needs, I set to work with the space planning.

At the first concept meeting, I knew we were in trouble. Barry, a wine importer and art collector, was remarkably relaxed about the technical details. "Sure, that wall is fine there, but which piece from my latest art collection will be best suited in that western exposure?" Carrie was as close to opposite as you could get. As a scientist for the U.S. government, she cared only for the stats of the pitch. "Barry, concentrate! If we push back this other wall 3 1/8 inches, we potentially gain an extra square foot in the bath-

room!" Armed with detailed notes for the second round of drawings, I returned to my studio. Soon after, I received a phone call
from Carrie that went a little something like this:

"Leslie," she whispered. "Yes, Carrie?" "You
know the door wall we talked about closest to the
stairs?" she said quietly. "Well, move it back 3 1/8
inches! The hallway needs to be wider, so just do
it!" "Why are we whispering, Karen?" I replied.
"Tsk. Because Barry is in the other room!"

Ten minutes later I receive this email from Barry:

> Hey Les, I hope you're enjoying our project
> and the amazing potential it has. I just opened
> a 2007 Beaux Freres Pinot Noir and was so
> inspired by the beauty of the label that I wanted to tell you
> my idea right away! The door wall we talked about—I think
> it should be brought forward about a foot closer to the stair-
> case so that we can hang vintage labels that I'm going to have
> framed! How amazing will that be!?!??!?

Typically I'd say it's a good thing to have one person concerned
with the aesthetics of a project and one to pay attention to the
overall function. Balance is good (all praise balance in relationships). The extremes of both partners, however, prevented each

Spouses with differing personalities and design styles benefit from having a designer as a referee who can interpret all spousal needs and create a cohesive plan.

of them from seeing the project holistically and appreciating the other's viewpoint, which makes my job as the designer nearly impossible.

The second concept meeting with Barry and Carrie started out less productively and slightly more hostile than the first. I had blended their needs as much as possible with the newest set of plans, but each still reverted to their own ideas of perfection as we talked through the layout. When their comments devolved into a Springer-esque shouting match, I knew I had to act to save their project (and potentially their marriage).

According to the National Health Statistics Report, a married couple divorces every 13 seconds in the United States. The top two reasons cited are poor communication and financial troubles.

Here's the thing: *I'm not a marriage counselor.* I'll gladly take on a bad-boy floor plan and reform the hell out it, but please, please listen to the nice designer as I say that I don't want to be the referee in your marital spats. As I sat in that pitch meeting and realized that Barry and Carrie were paying me to listen to them argue, I quietly gathered my things and stood up. Bingo: silence. Having their attention, I said "what we have here is an abundance of opinions, and an absence of communication. I need you both to make a decision now regarding whether you really want this project to happen, because we're only in the planning stages and you're ready to kill each other. As much as I love y'all as individuals, I can't take sides when we get to court and the prosecutor asks me whether the deceased spouse had it coming."

Barry laughed. His reaction broke the tension, and Karen touched his hand. They looked at each other, then me, and confirmed their desire to continue the project. "Okie dokie," I said, "let's go about this in a different way." I handed each of them a blank piece of paper and a marker, and pointed to different rooms for them to sit and complete an assignment. "Make two columns for me," I began. "In the first column, put the name of the friends that you're enticing to visit at the top. Under that, make a list of the five most important elements of the remodel to make your friends happy. The second column can be filled with adjectives to describe the new space—describe how it will look, feel, and work. Keep in mind your audience when you're developing the list; if your friends will be the only ones using the space, then have the courtesy of making it about *them*, not about you."

Having a "safe word" is helpful in preventing heated arguments during remodel planning. Agree on a word that signifies immediate cease fire so you can both calm down and refocus.

The results were fascinating. I had them rejoin me in the kitchen where I privately compared their lists. I nodded with approval when I saw the expected results, then handed them back. "Now swap papers," I said, channeling my 6th grade math teacher. "Let's grade." The result: A+ for both students. When I took away Barry and Carrie's own neuroses about the project and made them pay attention to the user (their visiting friends), the lists were identical. While the order of the list may have differed, every element matched. Hooray! A common goal without painful compromise or bloodshed!

Knowing the Plan

Barry and Carrie were lucky that they didn't have to compromise on their master list of requirements for the remodel—their vision of the project was well-aligned, and simply suffered from lack of proper communication. Realistically, when spouses take on a project, compromise is absolutely required. Bloodshed is NOT. Outside factors like budget, contractors, and materials can sometimes be the source of need to compromise, but proper communication and planning can prevent homicide. So how do you properly communicate and plan a remodel project? Let's start with these four key elements:

Remodeling is about fixing homes, not people.

KNOW YOUR ROLE

Carrie was a numbers gal and wanted to be responsible for all things money related. It helped her to feel in control of the project and kept her artistic husband in check. On the flip side, Barry was all about the aesthetics and did a fabulous job of ensuring that the space had tons of personality. Consider your natural strengths and plan for the role that you and your spouse or family will play during the remodel. Make sure that EVERYONE involved is, well, involved. Remodeling is about fixing homes, not people.

KNOW IT'S GONNA SUCK

I'm not going to lie to you and tell you remodeling is easy. It's just not. There is no such thing as a painless, quick, stress-free project. You can prepare well, you can go with the flow, you can have a great partner and a fantastic design and build team that will make your life as easy as possible during the process, but that's honestly the best you can expect. I promise you this though: If you plan and communicate well, it'll be all right in the end, and if it's not all right, it's not the end.

KNOW YOUR AUDIENCE

If you know that you are a zombie before coffee in the morning, don't engage in important conversations about the project until you're properly caffeinated. If you know from experience that your partner isn't a good listener after 8pm, choose a time before then

> **Han•ger**
> **[hang-ger], noun**
> The anger one feels due to extreme hunger causing extreme asshole-ish behavior until calories are consumed.

to bring up important details. If you know your kids have raging hanger before dinner, don't ask them for input on your project until they're fed. Knowing your audience is an important key in effective communication.

KNOW WHEN IT'S TIME

Major life events are often the catalyst for home improvement. Births, deaths, marriages, divorces, and aging in place issues are all excellent reasons to remodel to your home. Many of my clients have come to me after traumatic life changes looking to completely renovate. The clients who had sought therapy were encouraged to wait six months before making major life decisions, but every case is different. One client waited twenty minutes after a major event to start planning changes. Another waited six years. Think carefully about why you want to remodel and consult a therapist if needed.

Knowledge is power. Understanding the importance of these four elements as you begin to plan your remodel will help make your project more successful. We'll use the lessons from Barry and Carrie along with other client stories throughout this book to illustrate a variety of communication issues and how they impact a remodel project.

You know you're ready to move on when......

You and your spouse have had a lengthy (preferably sober) conversation about the need for a remodel and have discussed and agreed upon the four key elements of knowing your role, knowing it's going to suck, knowing your audience and knowing when it's time.

do:
make brain

The Brain

Now that you're in the know about the big four elements, it's time to get serious about planning and making the project real and tangible. We'll accomplish this task by making THE BRAIN.

THE BRAIN is your first planning assignment. Now that you're mentally prepared with the big picture of remodeling realities, it's time to get your shit together so we can create order out of alllll the paper stuffs you're about to be inundated with during the remodeling process. Having watched clients search for a solid twenty minutes through piles of random papers in their home for a spec sheet that an appliance salesperson gave them weeks before, I can guarantee you that you'll thank me later for making you create one central location for All Things Remodelish now. Those documents should live in a binder called THE BRAIN in an agreed-upon place in your home. Ready to do some work?

In order to apply for an internship at HDD, students must answer the following question: "HDD is located near a Civil War-era cemetery. In the event of a zombie apocalypse, what practical skills would you offer the Hart-Davidson Designs team for our survival and protection as a group?

HDD

My hella-organized clients keep a binder for their projects with specific sections for pre-planning, inspiration pictures, bids, contracts, business cards, spec sheets, appliance manuals, warranties, and annnnnything else that would fit in the All Things Remodelish category. I love those clients.   I especially loved when one of those clients went to fetch the binder during a meeting from the usual place she kept it and discovered it missing. "BRAIN! BRAINNNNZZZZ" she yelled as she ambled zombie-like through the house to find where her husband had accidentally left it.

It's up to you how your BRAIN is compartmentalized. I've used an example from a kitchen remodel to show you common sections. The homework and worksheets I'll ask you to complete in the upcoming chapters like to live in the BRAIN for easy reference. If you're thinking "Hey, tree killer! Why can't I do all this digitally, huh?," no worries. I'm not advocating paper-only for the reference material, but I guarantee you'll get a ton of tangible bits along the way whether you like it or not, and they've gotta go somewhere. Make a BRAIN folder on your computer for things you collect digitally along the way as well.

Interns are revered at HDD. Since 2006, HDD has mentored over 100 interns from Michigan State University whose brilliant ideas constantly keep me on my toes.

HDD

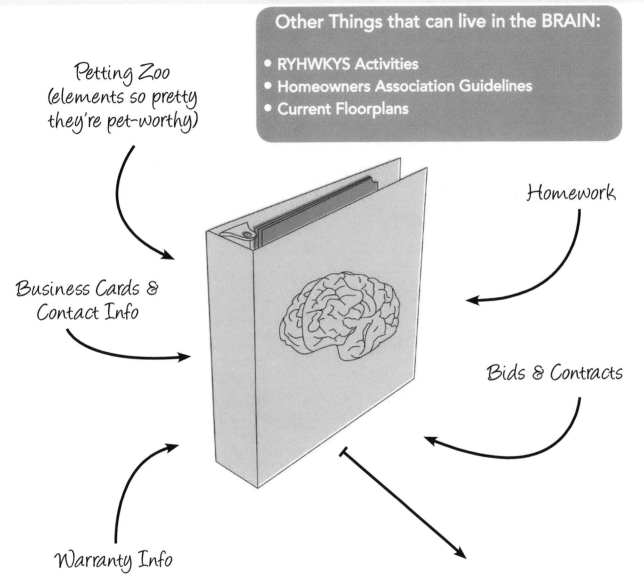

Other Things that can live in the BRAIN:

- RYHWKYS Activities
- Homeowners Association Guidelines
- Current Floorplans

Petting Zoo
(elements so pretty
they're pet-worthy)

Homework

Business Cards &
Contact Info

Bids & Contracts

Warranty Info

Look for this icon throughout the book.
It will help you know that its an activity
that lives best in the BRAIN.

Space Shaming

"Fat-shaming." "Dog-shaming." "Slut-shaming." "Toddler-shaming." The genre of shaming continues to grow in both style and absurdity, so I'll throw my shaming hat in the ring with this little doozy: Space-shaming. Firmly centered between the malice of Fat-shaming and the dysfunction of Toddler-shaming, the concept of Space-shaming allows the users of a space to easily blame every woe and wrongdoing wholly and completely on the space itself without any culpability of the users.

Time and time again, I have witnessed clients with shaky relationships who regularly communicate ineffectively with each other readily blame the space in their home instead of looking inward for answers. It's much easier to blame your crappy relationship on a poorly designed existing work triangle in a kitchen than it is to talk about why you routinely argue with your spouse in that space. Having a more functional kitchen won't prevent you from yelling at your spouse when he arrives late for dinner or ignoring your wife all evening because she bought the wrong flavor of Chobani yo-

SPACE SHAMERS

gurt. Trust me: marriage counseling is a hell of a lot cheaper than remodeling, so take a good hard look at your relationship and figure out your beef with your spouse before you Space-shame and enter into one of the most stressful experiences of your life: remodeling. To better understand the impact of Space-shaming, let's take a look at a couple that employed this shaming technique with such prowess that they actually caused me PTSD: Post-Traumatic Stress Design. We'll call them The Flitters.

STORYTIME: THE FLITTERS

Mrs. Flitter, a yoga instructor, worked hard to maintain a persona of lightheartedness and fun that was infectious. Mr. Flitter presented as a gregarious fellow who wanted a hand in all the action. I can tell you that after a year of working with the Flitters, I had suffered from enough PTSD to make me rethink my profession.

The trouble started the first time I met with the Flitters. Pinning them down on an exact style was like herding cats: messy, unproductive and full of battles. Just when we assumed we had locked in all the selections, the Flitters would throw a curveball. "What if we take out all the soffits?!?!" they asked excitedly. "Well, that's like scheduling a mammogram and coming out with a boob job," I explained patiently. "It's invasive, costly and time consuming. You don't have the time or the budget to do it, so I strongly recommend against it."

Despite my warning, they decided to have me work it into the plan. I became nervous as the multiple design concept meetings proved that the Flitters were not communicating with each other apart from our meetings. In fact, the Flitters seemed unable to answer basic questions about their own usage in the kitchen and were only concerned about the flow of people during parties and bigger events. During one meeting, the Flitters staged my crew as "party guests" and attempted to explain their need for function in the kitchen as they accessed the refrigerator, stove and sink with the extra bodies in the way.

After the functional layout was resolved, it took a record-setting SIX appointments to select materials and finishes. I would bring in all the new samples and drawings, lay them out in place, turn to the Flitters and explain using sound design principles why THIS new design would work. Each time there was assurance that I had nailed it with this selection, it looked great, and they were ready to sign the contract and get started. I would leave feeling nauseated, counting down the hours until I would get an email or text saying "I'm juuuuust not sure about...." Mrs. Flitter had issues of commitment to materials the way Larry King had issues of commitment to his seven wives. Despite my constant reassurance, there was always something missing from the materials I presented her. On the sixth reselect, I informed Mrs. Flitter that a choice would need to be made as the possibility for dragging this on for the rest of her natural life was imminent.

The contract was finally signed and the project began in earnest. From the first day of construction, I would receive duplicate texts and emails from both Flitters anywhere from 7am to midnight. It was clear while talking on the phone with one Flitter that the other Flitter hadn't been informed of a recent decision or plan. One evening, I could hear the back-and-forth as Mrs. Flitter relayed info to her husband while talking with me. At one point after Mrs. Flitter explained a term incorrectly to her spouse, Mr. Flitter grabbed the phone from her, yelled at her for being stupid, then demanded I repeat the information. The phone fight lasted ten minutes as Mr. Flitter worked through all his rhetorical (and marital) issues. Mrs. Flitter would pass off his awful behavior each time she recovered possession of the phone to talk to me. "He just had a rough day at work, dear. He didn't mean to yell or to call anyone stupid, DID YOU HONEY?" she demanded.

> **"He just had a rough day at work, dear. He didn't mean to yell or call anyone stupid, DID YOU HONEY?"**

During my last site visit, I took a metaphorical knife to the heart upon hearing this statement from Mrs. Flitter: "We're just not happy in this kitchen." I looked around carefully at a beautiful, flawless, perfectly functional magazine-worthy kitchen and wondered if Mrs. Flitter said the same thing about her infant to the obstetrician after giving birth. It was clear that the Flitters used space-shaming to the highest degree: with a perfectly lovely kitchen that met

EVERY SINGLE ONE of their requirements for design and ended up being a notch above the original aesthetic selections, they STILL felt unhappy in the space. The space, however, lived up to its end of the deal. If the Flitters worked as hard at communicating with each other as they did at shaming their space, they'd have the best marriage on the block.

While the Flitters were unwilling to look inward for answers to their unhappiness, the next couple who started on a path of easy Space-shaming ultimately turned their gaze toward their relationship and discovered something pretty incredible in the process. Let's call them the Futons.

STORYTIME: THE FUTONS

Mrs. Futon was a physician who loved her four young children dearly. She and Mr. Futon, a small business owner, had moved into a fabulous and schwanky new construction community several years before. They brought with them their college furniture in-cluding a creaky, stained futon that sat awkwardly in a formal living room with soaring ceilings. "We never made it to the grown-up phase," Mrs. Futon explained. "Since the kids were little, we de-cided to just let them beat up this furniture until we were ready to be adults and, ya know, have people over and stuff. We're ready." The dorm-style furniture wasn't the only indication that the couple hadn't fully emotionally invested in the new home: there were no pictures on the wall, no family photos, no meaningful décor any-where that helped me determine who they were and how I could help them live better in their home. In fact, when I gave them the fire test (you'll learn about this on page 160 of the Character sec-tion), the results suggested that they were treating their residence more like a hotel than a home.

Throughout the interview process with the Futons, my questions about the scope of work and their wishes for my involvement began to show bigger issues. "The space just feels so cold," Mrs. Futon would explain. "I just want to be happy when I come home," Mr. Futon offered. During the questions, the kids gathered and were routinely hugged and doted on by Mrs. Futon. There was no doubt that she loved them fiercely and wanted them to feel comfortable in the space. There was also no doubt that she and Mr. Futon had completely different design aesthetics based on their responses to my inquiries about color, furniture, finishes, and style. I had my work cut out for me.

> The inability to compromise over design style can be a deal breaker. Consider choosing rooms that each spouse has creative control over to prevent constant battles.

A few months into the design process that left my brain hurting from so much stylistic compromise, I received a shocking email from Mrs. Futon explaining that she and Mr. Futon had filed for divorce. "So the kids and I are staying in the house, and I need to change everything we've discussed so far. I'm sorry, but at the same time I'm not. Are you still in?"

> **Sometimes, it's the person IN THE SPACE with you, not the space itself that is causing unhappiness.**

Hell yeah, I was in. Mrs. Futon did the design equivalent of lifting a leg and peeing on the elements that she loathed from her compromise with Mr. Futon. After we finished the designs and started construction, she confided in me that for the first time in her life, she was going to come home to a house filled with nothing but love. "This is really me now," she said. "I thought that fixing the emptiness of the house would fix the emptiness of my marriage, but I was wrong."

Mrs. Futon was a magnificent client and continues to be a friend to this day. I silently cheered the day she told me she figured out why the house felt empty and wished that all of my clients had that kind of clarity and introspection. For the record: if you're arguing with your spouse about your space, I'm not advocating divorce. Divorce is shitty and painful—trust me, I watched my folks battle for years. I'm simply asking that you look hard enough to find the source of your unhappiness before you let the space take the fall for your current misery. Sometimes, it's the person IN THE SPACE with you, not the space itself that is causing unhappiness.

Space Shaming Hall of Fame

Creepiest FUTURE Relationship

A divorced guy in his mid 40's hired me to design the interior of his lavish new construction home. He was completely up front about why he was building a large home instead of keeping his bachelor loft: "My loft will not attract the proper mate. This will serve me better as I woo a new wife," he explained nonchalantly while selecting roofing shingles. It became clear during subsequent walk-throughs of the construction site just how much he wanted a wife, and how specific he was being about that position: "The lady of the house will sit and write her thank-you notes at the balcony office overlooking the formal living room here" he proclaimed with a sweeping arm gesture. "In my loft, she would be too confined. That won't do."

Under my breath, I asked if she would need to rub the lotion on its skin as well. Luckily, he didn't hear that.

Space Shaming Hall of Fame

Hookup AIN'T Happening

A bachelor hired us to transform his sparse space into a home more reflective of his personality to impress dates. My staff and I spent over a year adding all the right elements to help him look like a great catch. After he became more comfortable with our team, he worked up the courage for another request: he wanted his unstylish bedroom to look as cool as the rest of his home. "All the women LOVE the main part of the house, but they're not impressed in the bedroom. It MUST be the décor that's turning them off. Can you fix that please?" "My team can fix the space," I explained. "But how you perform in it is…um….all on you." "Great!" he replied. "Here's a retainer check!"

Space Shaming Hall of Fame

Out WITH the OLD

A retired couple hired me to remodel their main floor to make it more accessible as they aged in place. The wife had been widowed for a decade and had recently married a long-time bachelor who moved into the home she had lived in for 30 years with her first husband. Husband #2 was quite opinionated about the design plans and intended to eradicate every memory and tangible reminder of husband #1 in the process. "This is ugly. This is worn out. This is dated." he commented as we walked through the home with the wife trailing behind. When we stood in the living room and stared at the impressive built-in bookcases that husband #1 had lovingly created by hand, #2 boldly declared "You need to just rip it all out!" The wife blanched, so I asked for her input. "I've always loved the style and they're quite functional," she answered meekly. The new husband turned red, yelled "It's ALWAYS SOMETHING of HIS!" and stormed out of the room. The wife ended up appeasing husband #2 by agreeing to tear out the bookcases, but I ended up appeasing the wife by secretly reusing all of the beautiful bookcase wood for column details in the living room.

do:
wish list

Wish List

Now that we've started building the BRAIN and ensuring you're not space-shaming your way into a remodel, let's start thinking about exactly what expectations you have for a new space. The first activity is to create a WISH LIST. There's only one rule with the wish list homework: NO CENSORSHIP. Just let your brain and your heart produce as much content as you'd like to best explain the wishes you have for you home. Remember when you were 7 and you wrote a wish list to Santa Claus a mile long? You knew there was no way in hell he was going to bring you everything, but you wrote it anyway. Again, don't worry about censoring yourself at first—just get it all out so you and your family can discuss the ideas. Do that now with your home remodeling wish list as you answer this question: **with a bottomless budget, what changes would you make to your home?**

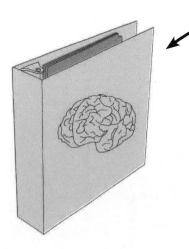

Put your uncensored Wish List in your BRAIN after you dis cuss it with you partner.

remodeling your house without killing your spouse

do:
T/NAT

Show and Tell

As much as your spouse and family would like to look inside your brain and see exactly what you're trying to describe as a style for your remodel, their powers of x-ray vision just aren't up to the task. Make life easier by assembling a grouping of THING/NOT A THING (or T/NAT) examples to be able to discover your own personal style and preferences. You have the option of collecting these examples of style tangibly in the form of magazine pages or prints from the web, or virtually through Pinterest. Knowing what you do and don't like about specific décor will be remarkably helpful in creating a remodeled space that you love. Here is the assignment for you and your family:

1. **Look for examples** of rooms or individual elements in magazine pages that you believe are either a THING or NOT A THING. Make a pile of the THING pages, including initial reactions of which particular element caused the happiness. Was it the lighting? The wall color? The furniture arrangement? On the flip side, make a pile of NOT A THING pages with the same level of detail. It's perfectly okay to have a page with both THING and NOT A THING elements, so don't worry if you can't find a perfect room example. (for reference, one of my clients used 15 pages to cobble together what her idea of a perfect THING was). Use post-it notes to list the comments on those

individual pages, making sure to list clearly at the top the idea of what made the T/NAT, then give more detail down below. Example:

> ### NAT: color green
>
> When I was 6 I puked up fruit cocktail in my nana's kitchen. The walls were that shade green and I've never been able to look at it without remembering blowing chunks against her wall.

2. **Place your pages in your BRAIN** under your own tab to review with your family. Everyone who regularly uses the space should participate in this homework and share the joy of T/NAT. If you've gone the virtual route, then create two Pinterest boards (hide them if you don't want to offend the previous pinner with a bigass "NOT A THING" tag) and use the comment section to properly describe the reaction as you would with post-it notes. Samples of THING/NOT A THING boards and homework along with thorough comments are available on the HDD Pinterest page under "designdemocracy".

Here are tips for productive sharing and review of the T/NAT pages with your spouse or family:

• only allow one person at a time to do a T/NAT review. The tangible pages get too jumbled up and overwhelming if there is more than one pile, and the dueling computer screens will make you hear the theme song from Deliverance in your head.

• encourage the T/NAT review to be as subjective and opinionated as possible. The only way to truly discover a personal style is to be...well....personal. Don't try to sugar-coat the unsavory elements at this point in the process. If you don't make your opinions known now, you'll pay for it mid-remodel when you discover that you forgot to tell your spouse that you hate the color green.

• be as productive as possible with the narrowing of styles discovered in the T/NAT homework. If you notice that the idea line at the top of the postie note is consistent, you're on the right track to discovering your own personal style. If you don't see a pattern, try looking through different sources for more material and try again. It usually takes my clients about twenty pages to truly identify what they love and ultimately want to incorporate into their remodel.

What Your House CAN & CAN'T Do

Sometimes, décor is just décor. Sometimes, décor is a gateway drug to cure all that is wrong with your family. Clients can mistake the power of pillows or a giant tv to beckon, to calm, or to create fuzzy happy feelings in a space where there really are none. Unlike Space Shamers mentioned earlier in this chapter, these folks are well-intentioned and without malice towards their spaces. However, they often confuse the problem of "I can't get my family to _____" as one that can be solved with stuff instead of talking about their feelings. These next two stories illustrate precisely what happens when décor is used as a fix-all for behavior.

STORYTIME: PINKY VONPINKERSON

A frazzled mother once tried to convince herself that changing the pillows in the living room would make her children and spouse want to join her more often for quality time in what her family had dubbed "momland". The room in question could be more accurately described as the "Pepto Palace". This mythical place consisted of….well….pink. It looked as if a tanker truck full of Pepto Bismol backed up to the room and hosed down every vertical and horizontal surface.

The early 20th century invention of Pepto-Bismol coincided with other health advances in the US, such as public campaigns advocating hand washing and milk pasteurization. This trio of advances knocked infant diarrhea out of the top spot on the list of causes of infant death.

Every element in momland was of the pink and floral persuasion. What started out harmlessly as a donation of a light pink floral sofa from her mother-in-law turned quickly into a Vesuvian explosion of femininity that sent her mostly-male family running in the other direction. When Pinky VonPinkerson realized that her family was shunning the Pepto Palace and wouldn't join her in the room to watch tv and chat, she called me to assist.

"How do you want to feel when you walk into this room?" was my first question as I surveyed the pinkscape during the consultation. Mrs. VonPinkerson missed the point as she said "Oh, I feel great when I walk in here. I love it! You just need to convince my family that it's great, too." "So let me get this straight," I began. "You want me to confirm how lovely this room is to your family so they'll spend more time here?" "Precisely!" she responded. I hesitated, saying "and... you believe this will make them want to join you in here more?" I watched Pinky straighten the mauve velvet arm cover that I had leaned against. My eyes flicked from the lace curtain panels to the massive Hummel figurine collection to the meticulously arranged six-month display of Country Living magazines fanned out on the coffee table with precisely 1.75" of space between each periodical.

> **"You want me to confirm how lovely this room is to your family so they'll spend more time here?" "Precisely!" she replied.**

Pinky VonPinkerson's eyes followed my path around the room, and I saw her resolve begin to fade. "Well....." she began, "my sons say that the sofa pillows are a little too scratchy. Perhaps you can make some custom toss pillows that are velvet instead of lace?" I opened my mouth, but no sound came out.

I was reaching for a way to gently explain to Pinky that softer pillows would not successfully woo teenagers into the Pepto Palace when one of her sons arrived home from school. "My baby's home!" Pinky shouted, grabbing the startled teenager for a hug and planting huge smooches on his cheek, complete with sound effects. The poor kid turned as pink as the carpet while I witnessed the VonPinkerson reunion. While he was captive in his mother's embrace, I took the opportunity to interview him about momland.

"We all love her, but she's so neurotic about the room that we're afraid of sitting in there and making her fidget."

"Dude, what'll it take for you to make your mom happy and spend some time in here with her?" The son, still being squished by Pinky, wheezed his answer. "BULLdooOoozzzzZZ-er." Okay, not helpful. Another teenage son walked in, and Pinky released her first catch of the day to smother the second arrival. I continued the interview with the squished son and listened as he explained what the family would require to enter momland.

"It's totally over the top, and she just doesn't see it," Squishy began. "It was funny at first, wondering what else she could paint pink and stick in the room, but it just didn't stop. We all love her, but she's so neurotic about the room that we're afraid of sitting in there and making her fidget."

"I don't fidget," Pinky's singsongy voice replied as she moved the lace doily on the sofa table a quarter of an inch to the left. The two squished sons and I stared her down, my right brow rising to alarming heights, and Pinky realized her task. "Oh, dear," she said, sitting down on the upholstered Pepto piece that started the pastel riot. I could tell she struggled to hold back from realigning the magazines that her leg bumped as she dramatically sank to the sofa. I sat beside her, patted her knee, and whispered "it's not about the pillows." Her eyes met mine, and she nodded. "Your family loves you very much," I continued. "But if you want them to spend time in here with you, it needs to be a space that everyone will enjoy, including you. Your thoughts in here should be about the time you have with your family instead of the best polish to remove the watermark from a glass."

"Love Connection" host Chuck Woolery made the term "two and two" famous during his reign from 1983-1994 by describing the commercial break length with his popular flippy-peace-sign hand gesture.

I channeled Chuck Woolery as I spent more time with Pinky on a game plan to slowly transform the Pepto Palace into a welcoming space for all members of her family. I was pleased that the improved "love connection" between the VonPinkerson family made the kids struggle to find a new nickname for the redesigned living room. They were quick to describe the results: "It's not quite Switzerland, but at least it's not hostile anymore."

STORYTIME: THE CO-SLEEPERS

An insanely busy surgeon and his wife had been clients of mine for about a year when they assigned me the task of transforming their beloved daughter's bedroom from frilly little girl décor into to a respectable teenage space. "It's time," the doting mother said as she gave me a $40,000 budget for Suzy Sighsmore's room. "It's just time." As we flipped through trendy catalogs for inspiration during the first consultation, the parents envisioned a desk space where their good little girl would sit with her five tutors and fill her brain with ivy-league-worthy studies. The plan also included a custom window seat for reflecting on the prose of great philosophers, an entertainment unit with a 40" LED television to watch only "educational" dvds, and a queen-sized bed with twenty custom pillows to rest her weary eyes after a long, productive day of academic achievement (but hey—that's no pressure on a 13 year old).

Yes, I give all clients funny nicknames. It's a THING to help us differentiate the projects in the HDD studio.

Suzy Sighsmore seemed mildly interested in the selection of the furniture pieces for her room and would make a good show of agreeing with her parents when it came to the functionality of the furniture, but she was not digging the overall plan. At several points in conversation, Suzy would sigh, then say "guys, really, you don't need to buy me things" punctuated by another sigh. When the parents refused to listen, Suzy tried again: "This isn't necessary. Seriously. <sigh>"

Despite the conflict, I continued with the design and execution while trying to extract as much input from Suzy as possible. When the big reveal came, her friends and extended family loved the new look. I crossed my fingers that Suzy would find the room functional and beautiful as well.

I followed up with the parents a few weeks later to see how Suzy was enjoying the new space. The mother hesitated to answer when I called her, but finally gave me some critical information that she failed to divulge at the start of the project: after the big reveal party, Suzy (as was custom for the last 13 years of her life) crawled in bed with her mother. Her father worked nights, so her mother had welcomed Suzy in the bed with her since she was a toddler to keep her company. The goal of the pricey bedroom remodel was to entice Suzy to sleep in her OWN bed for

"Oh, wait - you wanted me to SLEEP IN THERE?"

the first time in her life. "Oh, wait—you wanted me to SLEEP IN THERE?" Suzy replied when her mother told her co-sleeping would stop as of that night.

Suzy had told me this when I talked to her during the followup visit: "I do my homework in the kitchen. I watch tv in the family room. I read in the living room. I sleep in my mom's room. Why would I want my own space? I tried to tell them, but they didn't listen."

Suzy Sighsmore's parents didn't consult with their daughter about the true purpose of the bedroom remodel. Ignoring the co-sleeping problem by throwing cash and décor at it certainly didn't help, but a free conversation might have easily solved the problem. Oh, and if you're wondering, I did get an update recently: Suzy left for college having never slept in her own room.

What can we learn from the VonPinkersons and the Co-Sleepers?

1. **You can't buy love with décor.** In Pinky's case, the Pepto Palace was a great reflection of her own personal taste, but it most certainly didn't appeal to the teenage sons. It's totally fine to have a space that is alllll about you, but don't expect your family to join you there and love it in the same way.

2. **You can't solve problems without addressing the issues.** Pinky and the Co-Sleepers both completely overlooked the bigger picture and took the easy way out to solve their problems—Pinky

tried replacing the pillows and the Co-Sleepers pimped out the kid's room. These covert attempts backfired for both families. If you want behavior to change, you have to address the particular behavior.

3. **You can't ignore your family's feedback.** When Suzy Sighsmore told her parents quite clearly that they didn't need to buy her things for her room, they failed to listen. The result was an unnecessary $40,000 expenditure that could have been easily prevented with a single productive conversation.

Home CAN

- Be a refuge
- Be a perfect representation of your heritage, faith, and personalities (who you are, where you come from, and what you believe in)
- Be a basis for growth and reflection of your family

Home CANNOT

- Make you love it if you don't invest effort in the relationships with the people living there
- Make you happy simply by filling it with crap
- Make your kids stay present and out of trouble

remodeling your house without killing your spouse

do: current reality

Current Reality

It's time to take a good hard look at your current reality at home. You can't move forward successfully until you identify where you are right now, so think about the truths of your situation before you jump into remodeling.   It's easiest to start with the factual items first before launching into the emotional component, so here are some examples: the house is 2000 sq feet, which is a decent size. The neighborhood is great. The kitchen appliances are old and need to be replaced. The bathroom smells like a boys' locker room and the stench won't go away. The kitchen cabinet drawers are falling apart and I want to throw the jenky pieces of shit across the room on a daily basis. My spouse is cheap and won't spend what I want on the quality materials for this remodel.

See? Facts soften the blow before the emotional content begins. Take time to list your current reality with these questions. When you are done, share them with your family and place this list in the BRAIN.

List your current reality to identify areas of concern:

- What spaces work or not, and why?
- Do you have enough space?
- Do you have the right kind of space?
- Is the house in the right neighborhood or location?
- Are there structural or maintenance issues to consider?

remodeling your house without killing your spouse

Function

User testing is a THING. For many days, be an observer in your own home to get a good grip on the functional aspect of your space. As a designer, my key factor of success in a project is ensuring that whatever I create will not only look great, but also WORK. Nothing sucks more than going through the stress and enormity of remodeling only to discover that your new space isn't functional, so pay close attention to how your space functions (or doesn't) to add to the pro/con list in the next assignment.

Here are some examples of notes from clients who observed function and were rewarded with fabulous new spaces that worked perfectly.

Mud **ROOM**	Kitchen	Master **BEDROOM**
Need 2 more cubbies for backpacks and coats	Triangle is hella-dumb	Blinded by crappy overhead light
need an info center w/ family calendar	island is too short to be useful & in the way	comfy chair just holds laundry
location of door from garage is good	plenty of electrical outlets	Can't see tv from current bed location

Louis **SULLIVAN**

Architect Louis Sullivan's popular phrase "Form follows function" is of tremendous use in interior design for ensuring that the space not only looks good, but also performs well. Putting time and effort into a design for your space that ends up being attractive but not functional is like landing a dream date with a gorgeous model and discovering that the beautiful creature is vacuous, empty-headed and crappy at conversation: there's not a lot of *there* there.

Pro/Con Chart

Keep in mind at this point that you're still just investigating the idea of remodeling. There are other options to consider, and the honest responses that you and your partner give during this pro/con exercise will help decide what steps to take next. Think of it as a "choose your own adventure" task that can end in a multitude of ways: remodeling, moving, building, doing nothing, homicide, or divorce. Just kidding on the last two (mostly).

Use the chart on the next page to list both the pros and cons of your current home based on the opinions of your spouse and family. List aesthetic items, functional items, location, time frame, and any other element that will help you make this important decision.

Remember, all of the forms shown in RYHWKYS are available on the website at www.hddbook.com.

Pro/Con Chart

+	−

Sample Pro/Con Chart

	—
The natural light is great	Sink is too small
Kids enjoy doing their homework there	Island is small & in a jenky location
Plenty of storage	Tile countertop is hella-gross
	No place to store booze!

You know you're ready to move on when......

You listed more pros than cons. If not, remember this: it would suck to invest time and money into a project that you know will fail because of the overloaded con list that can't be salvaged by any amount of remodeling. Save the heartache and hand this book to someone else who can use it.

Acute vs. Chronic

Recognition of your home design problem is the first step in finding a viable solution with your spouse or partner. Living in the space daily can make that recognition either challenging or easy depending on the severity of the problem. Take for example our bodies and how we react to either acute or chronic pain. Developing arthritis and noticing that your range of motion has become more limited over the last few years is a chronic problem that you're likely to "get used to" or be able to ignore on certain days. A chronic design problem in a kitchen as a comparable example is cabinet drawers that creak, groan and stick as they slide out: you don't notice it until you use it, and some days (based on humidity and the season) are better than others.

An acute health problem such as appendicitis is similar to an epic home failure like the furnace breaking down or a home disaster. It needs to be addressed quickly for all systems to function properly. It's generally expensive to fix, takes a while to recover, and requires quick decision-making.

While chronically creaking drawers give you time to contemplate a new set of cabinets and layout for a kitchen remodel, an acute home-related issue requires quicker thinking. In either situation, it's easy to get lost in the multitude of options and decisions, resulting in fights with your spouse.

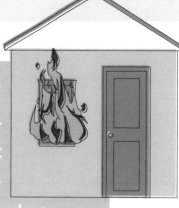

> Many folks take the opportunity to upgrade when faced with insurance claim work, but check with your agent about extra expenses or penalties for upgrading rather than just replacing what was lost.

Special Considerations

Democracy with the FAMILY: DESIGNING WITH KIDS

The birth of the Pottery Barn Teen catalog in 2003 gave credibility and a vehicle to joyful parents all across the U.S. who had been struggling for a decade to keep a leash on their teens. The furnishings and lifestyles promoted in the PB Teen catalog allowed these concerned (dare I say even "helicopter") parents to woo their walking hormonal progeny to hang out at their own house in order to keep a close eye on their socializing activities. Before PB Teen, parents would relegate the old family sofa to a basement, add a discarded television set and dvd player, stick a Nintendo on the coffee table, and be done with it. After PB Teen, the competition for the coolest hangout became ruthless. It wasn't just an old sofa anymore; it

> **Hel·i·cop·ter par·ents**
> [hel-i-kop-ter] [pair-uhnt], noun
> Over-involved parents who hover near their offspring and constantly fear for their daily safety and continue to manage the daily lives of their children well into college are referred to as "helicopter parents".

remodeling your house without killing your spouse

became an entire sectional in a washable bright-colored slipcover. It wasn't just the old tv; it became an entire entertainment unit with a 48" flat-screen LED display and a dvd collection that rivaled the daily stock of Netflix. It wasn't just a Nintendo; it became a highly-prized XBox gaming system with every imaginable accessory that required camping out in line at stores for hours for the honor of throat-punching other patrons to purchase it.

In the last decade, teen social spaces have evolved from total family cast-off furnishings and a plea from parents to "please, please bring your friends and hang out over here" to a whopping $20,000+ investment in infrastructure, décor and accessories and a plea from parents to "please, please let us be the coolest hangout on the block so I know my sweet baby is alive and *not* up to no good".

Before you make the big investment in bribing your offspring to hang out at your home, take a lesson from the Co-Sleeper story and humor me by talking to your kid. Knowing your audience is the first battle in any home improvement project, so start off right by doing your homework. The conversation would go something like this: "Dude, if I tricked out the basement and put in an Xbox and a snack bar, would you and your friends hang here?" If the answer is yes, then start earning your frequent flier miles on your credit card. If the response is no, then congratulate your kid for being honest (turn

> **Knowing your audience is the first battle in any home improvement project.**

down an Xbox? Are you serious?!?!). So what is it that they value more than cool spaces with gaming systems? Freedom.

I interviewed the teenage son of a client who had her heart broken after he turned down the offer to make a cool basement hangout. "It's not that I don't appreciate it," Teddy Turnitdown began. "But I already like my room and really don't need anything else." He thought for a second, then carefully looked around to see if his mom was lurking. Before I had a chance to tell him what a fine, upstanding, non-materialistic young man he was, Teddy added "but seriously, she wouldn't leave me alone if we had a space like that. Mom would find a million reasons to keep checking on us, and about the tenth time she told me to get my feet off the new sofa or use coasters for our drinks, my friends would get pissed and leave. She just doesn't get the idea that we want to hang out and not have her hover and check in like we're five and gonna set the house on fire. Yeah, it would be cool to have a bunch of new stuff, but not at that price."

> **Double Sided Expectations:**
> Discuss what the rules are for:
> • how the space is treated by the kids and
> • how the kids are treated in the space.

Remember Suzy Sighsmore and the epic $40,000 waste of money on her bedroom? That's another example of how parents fail at trying to control the behavior and actions of their kids through re-modeling. Stuff alone won't often keep kids home and safe, but communication and autonomy frequently will. Carefully interviewing your kid and making them part of the planning process from the start will give them an opportunity to be more invested in the project and ultimately use and care for it more than just ambushing them with a pricey project and shiny new toys and expecting positive results. Take the lessons from Teddy Turnitdown and Suzy Sighsmore and talk to your kids before you remodel.

AGING IN PLACE

Many of my senior clients have mentioned a need to address aging in place issues. Whether the comment is an innocuous "oh, I better install some grab bars in the bathroom" or a bigger concern of "let's talk about a large shower with no lip to make it easier for my folks to come and stay," it's important to consider all aspects of functionality and usability when it's time to remodel. If your five or ten year plan involves a change in mobility for either you or a family member, take time to check out all the resources available to design your space well and make the most of your remodel.

nahb.org

National Association of Home Builders (NAHB) provides a directory of Certified Aging in Place Specialist (CAPS) contractors who have been trained to address the many issues of accessibility and make spaces as useful and comfortable as possible for folks who want to stay in their homes.

nkba.org

National Kitchen and Bath Association (NKBA) provides a directory of Certified Kitchen Designers (CKD). Many of these designers have continuing education credits in both accessibility and aging in place issues and can assist with designing a fully functional kitchen or bath to suit your specific age-related needs.

acl.gov

The Department of Health and Human Services created the Administration for Community Living (ACL) to help the aging population to live at home with the support they need. The ACL website has links to resources for eldercare, benefits, and programs that assist in the process of aging in place.

A quick way to improve the usability and safety for elders in your home is to replace all knob-shaped door handles with an easy-open lever style.

remodeling your house without killing your spouse

Big Picture, Little Picture

Many clients are too vague when it comes to the reason for the remodel consultation. Stating that "My house just doesn't work for my family" or "My wife and I just aren't comfortable in this space" doesn't help either of us make a productive plan for the changes, so it's time to think big picture/little picture instead of being mired in complainy vagueland.

First, tell me this: why did you pick up this book? Did you like the cover and get sucked in by the funny stories and the foul language? Did you want to know what the bacon-haired designer was going to say about homicide during home improvement? Or did you think about the eleventy billion reasons you dislike your current space and want to change it without murdering your significant other in the process? I'm sure the last bit had *something* to do with your interest, so channel those reasons of space dislike into something more productive and start thinking big picture.

The big picture is essentially your goal for the remodel that could be stated as efficiently as possible. If a nosy neighbor stopped you while you carried in a heavy load of groceries and said "Hey, whatcha doin' in there?" how would you reply? That's the sort of big picture goal that should be listed.
Side note: "Ohh...ya know...remodeling" is an unacceptable an-

do:
goal

swer for both the nosy neighbor and the big picture sheet. You know you have to give the neighbor enough dirt to shut him up so you can get inside fast. Otherwise, he'll play twenty questions and trap you until the Haggan Daaz melts, and that would be tragic.

Remodel Goal:

Keep this front and center in the BRAIN to help remind you of the big picture goal when the remodel gets tough!

remodeling your house without killing your spouse

Communication Conclusion

Congratulations on completing the first section of Remodeling Your House without Killing Your Spouse! Before we move on to the very touchy subject of money, let's get our poop in a group and review the contents of your BRAIN. I'll sing the Bill Cosby "Picture Pages" song while you go gather all the goods. Ready?

At this point, your BRAIN should be in a central location with divider tabs for the "do" assignments for both spouses. We'll be adding more tabs shortly, but here is what should be completed and stored so far:

- wish list for remodel
- THING/ NOT a THING examples for each person
- current reality
- function test
- pro/con chart
- remodel goal (featured prominently in front)

At age 2, my daughter discovered my lack of musical talent and looked up at me while I sang the ABCs to her. "No, mama. NO SING!" she said stemly.

Remember that all of the forms in the book can be accessed through the Remodeling Your House without Killing Your Spouse website: www.hddbook.com.

Stop for a hot minute and think very hard about your remodel project as it relates to your relationship. If you have ANY hesitation about continuing the process, then have a frank conversation with your partner about your specific concerns and decide how you want to proceed.

The WORST thing you could do right now is plow ahead and ignore any of these red flags from your partner: refusing to do the exercises and homework, not listening to your opinions and ideas, or worse—arguing with you about the project. Please trust me when I tell you that I'd rather see you work on your relationship than your house. It doesn't make for a happy life when you have a fabulous new space, but the cost was learning that your spouse is an asshole.

You know you're ready to move on when......

You've completed your assignments without bloodshed or threat of divorce. More specifically, moving on to the cash section requires meaningful and productive conversations with your spouse about the following key concepts:
- recognizing that remodels fix homes, not people
- ruling out Space-shaming as project motivation
- understanding what your home can and can't do
- contemplating kid/aging special considerations
- agreeing on the big picture goal for the remodel
- assembling the brain with completed worksheets

cash

do

> 66 'That's an ambitious remodel list,' I told them. 'What's your budget?' 'We have $10,000' they replied. 'Add a zero.' I said. 99

learn

enjoy

Money Talk

Remember the Seinfeld episode where Kramer's landline is mistaken for Moviefone? Kramer takes delight in being the source of all movie listing knowledge, but finds the "press the first three letters of the movie you'd like to see" touch tones too hard to interpret. "Why don't you just TELL ME what movie you'd like to see!" he finally says. Kramer is able to stop guessing and start answering when the responses he receives are clearly spoken requests instead of misunderstood tones.

When it comes to budgets, I have Kramer-esque interactions like this frequently with clients as we embark on major remodels. When I first met with Barry and Carrie, we had the following conversation about their second floor remodel:

Me: "What's your budget?"
Client: "Well, what will it cost?"
Me: "That depends on your budget."
Client: "But what does an average remodel like this cost?"
Me: "About as much as a new car."
Client: "What kind of car?"
Me: "Exactly."

I understand that remodeling and car purchasing are whole different ballgames, but the concept is similar: you'd never walk into a car dealership and be cagey about what vehicle you want and what you're willing to pay. There's an expectation that car pricing varies significantly by make, model and features selected. Remodeling is the same: the pricing varies significantly based on scope, structural changes and tangible elements selected. You wouldn't walk into a Mercedes dealership wanting the newest model with premium upgrades knowing that you had more of a Honda budget, so give your remodeling contractor the same courtesy of having a firm number in mind of what you're willing to invest in your home before inviting them over for a consultation. It will make everyone's job easier when you have hard numbers instead of Kramer-esque touch tones.

During coy money conversations with clients who are unwilling or unable to give me firm dollar amounts for their project, I often start with this question: "What is the budget amount that would make you say 'holy shit, there's no way I'm spending that amount' and what is the budget that would make you say 'Ohh! That's not so bad.'" The number smack in the middle of those two answers is a good budget.

"Financial Fights are NOT a THING. Money doesn't lie, so talk with your spouse about what you can comfortably afford before you start planning in detail.

Being prepared for the budget question with your contractor is critical to the success of your project, but being prepared to have the budget conversation with your *partner* is critical to the success of your marriage. You and your spouse need to be on the same page about the major investment in your home. The time to talk about budget is NOT in front of your contractor at the first meeting. Be honest with each other about the comfort zone of cash before bringing others into the mix.

Budget vs. Reality

Cost can be a mystery when it comes to home improvement, and popular television shows are doing homeowners a tremendous disservice when it comes to informing their viewers of realistic costs for major projects. I am often forced to go to my happy zen place to prevent throwing the remote at the tv when I see hosts of remodeling shows boast how an entire kitchen remodel (including stainless steel appliances, high-end cabinetry, granite countertops and removal of that pesky load-bearing wall) only cost $20,000. Horseshit. Reality television is often light on reality, so you can't believe the stated cost when the producers of the show have arranged for the donation of all the labor fees and many of the materials in exchange for sponsorship and advertising.

"What will that cost?" they asked. "Add a zero," I replied.

This warping of budget reality is a challenge for me during consultations. I once met with a sweet couple who had their heart set on a major first-floor renovation. Their wish list included a full kitchen remodel, removal of two 15' load-bearing walls, a floor-to-ceiling stone fireplace in the family room, relocation of windows and sliding glass doors, wood floors throughout, and all new furniture. These folks weren't visual either, so they requested a package that included slick fly-through CAD drawings with three different design options that would take 20+ hours to create. "That's an ambitious list," I told them. "What's your budget?" "We have $10,000, but we prefer you stay under that" they replied. I laughed, thinking they were joking. They looked confused. "You mean $10,000 isn't enough? That's a LOT of money. The remodeling show last night did a similar project for close to that budget, but we aren't even expecting all those fancy finishes. What will it cost?" they asked. "Add a zero," I replied.

For perspective: design fees alone for the scale of project these clients desired would have been over $10,000 - ten perccent of the overall budget.

The financial reality of remodeling is a mystery to most homeowners, and the glory of the pretty before-and-after projects into a thirty-minute show is an irresistible siren to many. Before you jump in to remodeling, consider these three reality checks that will undo some of the taint from television.

Reality Check

1 Household Expenses

Unexpected expenses often pop up during remodels, so be prepared to shell out cash above and beyond the contract amount. Kitchen remodels, for example, mean higher food costs from eating out more often. Temporary gaping holes in your home along with vampiric power tools will impact your energy bills. Drycleaning expenses will increase as insidious drywall dust lands everywhere. Your entertainment budget will also rise as you high-tail away from the noisy, chaotic construction at every opportunity for a reprieve in the mall with retail therapy or a movie.

2 Costly DIY Projects

If you have training and skill in some home improvement areas, yay for you. If you're simply cheap and want to save money, I do NOT recommend tackling a DIY project during a remodel. Be aware of these HIDDEN COSTS of DIY, both monetary and other:
• your DIY contribution could delay the contractor if you aren't timely
• you could violate local building codes and create potential issues with future insurance claims
•you could ruin your relationship with one jenky grout line that your spouse holds against you for eternity

3 Lengthy Financial Deals

Be proactive with financing and determine what loan amount your home qualifies for *before* inviting a contractor over to play. Home Equity Lines of Credit (HELOC loans) are the quickest and easiest route for funds if you are sitting on a ton of equity, but the process still takes valuable time. Talking to your bank or Credit Union about possibilities for financing early in the process will prevent heartache if you don't qualify for the funds needed or if the process takes so long that the contractor bumps your job.

Priority List

Once you've talked with your spouse and have established a budget for your remodel project, make a priority list of each space and modification desired along with any specific elements you absolutely must have using the established budget amount. Start with a quick list by room, then use the worksheets on the next page to complete the process. Each partner should create their own priority list in order to establish expectations and be ready to take action with the information.

Kitchen
- layout
- cabinets
- countertops
- refrigerator
- stove
- dishwasher
- microwave
- disposal
- sink
- faucet
- flooring
- lighting
- backsplash tile
- cabinet hardware
- paint

Bath ROOM
- vanity
- sink
- faucet
- shower
- tub
- tile
- showerhead
- toilet
- paint

Living ROOM
- sofa
- chairs
- flooring
- occasional tables
- tv stand
- bookcases or built-ins
- window treatments
- accessories

Sample Priority List

List your specific goal from the communication chapter goal-setting activity here. Keep it in mind as you make your priority list.

If an item is non-negotiable, check this box so everyone understands your love!

> **Remodel Goal:**
> ## basement hangout

n-n	rank	item	description	manufacturer	price
☐	3	sectional	PB "comfort" in gray twill	Pottery Barn	$3000
☐	1	home theater	65" LED w/surround sound	Samsung	$3500
☑	2	insulation	for both heat & sound	Owens Corning	$tbd
☐	5	carpet	TruSoft Twist w/ nice pad	stainmaster	$450sf
☐	4	snack area	cabinets like in kitchen	AristoKraft	$1000?

Rank these parts of the remodel by how important each is to you. It will be interesting to compare with your partner later on!

No worries! Exact pricing on some items isn't possible until a full design plan exists.

Remodel Goal:

n-n	rank	item	description	manufacturer	price
☐	—	_____	_____	_____	$ _____
☐	—	_____	_____	_____	$ _____
☐	—	_____	_____	_____	$ _____
☐	—	_____	_____	_____	$ _____
☐	—	_____	_____	_____	$ _____
☐	—	_____	_____	_____	$ _____
☐	—	_____	_____	_____	$ _____
☐	—	_____	_____	_____	$ _____
☐	—	_____	_____	_____	$ _____

Don't forget to print out any specification sheets to add to your brain as you are researching items for your lists.

Expectations for performance will help make better selections.

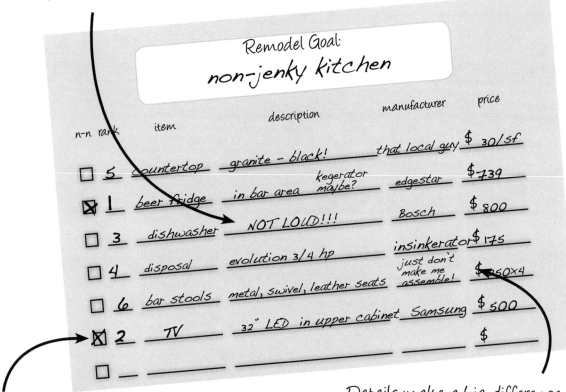

Remodel Goal:
non-jenky kitchen

n-n rank	item	description	manufacturer	price
☐ 5	countertop	granite - black!	that local guy	$ 30/sf
☒ 1	beer fridge	in bar area *kegerator maybe?*	edgestar	$739
☐ 3	dishwasher	NOT LOUD!!!	Bosch	$ 800
☐ 4	disposal	evolution 3/4 hp	insinkerator	$ 175
☐ 6	bar stools	metal, swivel, leather seats	*just don't make me assemble!*	$ 250x4
☒ 2	TV	32" LED in upper cabinet	Samsung	$ 500
☐				$

Wishes for function and use of the space will often be revealed in these priority lists. Be sure to discuss this at length with your partner.

Details make a big difference. Be honest about your tolerance for involvement. It might be worth the extra $ to have things installed or built for you.

CA-CHING!

Be up front about your non-negotiable items. The remaining budget will be established based on the cost of your favorite things.

n-n rank	item	description	manufacturer	price
☑ 1	gas stove	48" 6 burner	Five Star	$6247
☐ 3	farm sink	white porcelain - 36"	Kohler	$1290
☐ 2	countertop	quartz - black	Cambria	$60/sf ?? tbd
☐ 4	backsplash tile	multi-color glass	Tile USA	$30/sf
☐ 5	barstools	LEATHER! swivel	barstools.com	$250 x 4
☐ __	_____	_____	_____	$ ____

Remodel Goal: non-jenky kitchen

Your spouse might say, "what's a farm sink?" Have examples ready to show specific styles if the items are unfamiliar.

Searching alternate vendors is a great way to compromise on priorities. The element can stay the same, but the price can be reduced dramatically if you are willing to take the time to hunt for comparable items.

Taking Action with Priority Lists

Do you recall the story in the introduction about Barrie and Carrie? I intervened when they were miscommunicating and had them fill out individual priority lists with their remodel goal. When they finished, I asked them to swap papers to evaluate their partner's wishes for the project. Since the big picture goal was the same, it was easier for Barry and Carrie to ultimately compromise on the individual elements and move forward.

Once you have completed your priority list and have uninterrupted quality time to spend together, swap papers with your spouse and start talking about why you selected those elements for the project. Use spec sheets or other research materials to educate your spouse on a specific element if you know you'll encounter opposition. Being prepared to validate your choices of both functional and aesthetic items is key to moving forward in the remodeling project.

Home Im•prove•ment Professional [hohm] [im-proov-muhnt] [pruh-fesh-uh-nl], noun Home Improvement Professionals are specialists in the industry such as architects, contractors, designers and decorators.

When you can both agree on a priority list with the same specific elements for an established budget, it's time to seek out a home improvement professional.

Home Improvement Professionals

After you've had discussions with your spouse about the scope of your remodeling project and the details that are important to both of you, it's time to find a home improvement professional who can complete the work for a reasonable fee in a reasonable time frame with reasonable quality of work. Having your BRAIN binder out and ready along with all of the homework and activities completed to the best of your ability will show the home improvement professional that you mean business. You'll be ready to answer all of their questions about what you want done, what your budget is, and what your expectations are for the process. I can tell you from experience that clients who have their shit together and play nicely with each other during consultations tend to receive better pricing than clients who are vague, unprepared and impolite to their spouses. It is in your best financial interest to be well-prepared before calling a home improvement professional.

Fighting in front of a HIP will automatically increase your project costs if you're seen as a potential pain-in-the-ass.

Since you have devoted time and energy to preparing yourselves for the consultation, you should expect the same from your home improvement professional. There are many key players in the home improvement industry who can help you achieve certain aspects of your remodel, so let's take a look at who can do what to better identify which team player you should contact first.

architect   contractor

Architects ensure that walls & other structural bits don't buckle or collapse.

Hire me when you need to:
- have structural drawings made for the GC and building inspector
- change roof lines or move load-bearing walls
- make big (100 sq ft+) additions

Expect to pay:
$75-$150/hr or
5%-20% of overall project

Contractors build stuff and arrange for all trades to do their part for the remodel.

Hire me when you need to:
- Execute the structural plan from the architect
- Pull all necessary local permits and complete building inspections
- Complete any project above and beyond DIY skill level

Expect to pay:
A flat rate of markup that is built into the overall contract price

remodeling your house without killing your spouse

designer

decorator

Designers create functional, big picture plans and can implement the entire project.

Decorators make stuff pretty and pull all aesthetic elements together

Hire me when you need to:
- Create more detailed plans (kitchen & bath layouts) from architect's drawings
- Specify each fixture and finish for GC bid
- Wrangle the other players while implementing the plan

Hire me when you need to:
- Select paint colors
- Order window treatments
- Purchase furnishings and accessories

Expect to pay:
$75-$150/hr or
5%-20% of overall project

Expect to pay:
$50-$75/hr or
commission on each item

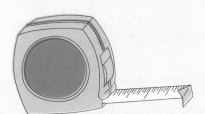

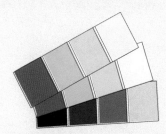

remodeling your house without killing your spouse

Playing Well With Others

Once you determine what kind of home improvement professional to hire, it's time to put on your human resources hat and get busy. Keep in mind that you'll be handing over what is likely your most valuable asset—your home—to a relative stranger who will have access to it at any time and bring through a string of other workers to rip the shit out of it during phase one and slowly rebuild it. Before you hand over a big-ass check and the key to your home, make absolutely sure that you understand the stakes and that you're 100% comfortable with the process.

I could easily spend 100 pages giving advice about how to locate, interview, vet, hire and work with this person, but I'll boil it down to the three critical points for the purpose of Remodeling Your House without Killing Your Spouse: choosing your dude, getting a solid contract, and proactively communicating.

Dude
[dood, dyood], noun
A generic term for any home improvement professional with no reference to gender, as in "yeah, I got a dude."

do:
choose your dude

> If you intend to wait a year before starting the remodel, don't call in a contractor and bait them with a great project, then say "ohhh, yeah, but we have to wait 12 months to save up money." That's just mean, and the pricing will fluctuate considerably. On the other hand, don't call them up and say "I want a new kitchen next week." (That won't happen. Ever.)

CHOOSE YOUR DUDE

There is a direct correlation between the kind of dude you hire and the kind of remodel experience you have. I've witnessed clients spend more time and effort selecting a $5 watermelon at a farmer's market than selecting the contractor who will potentially take a crap-ton of your money and have full access to your home and family. To make it easier for you, I've broken down the process into an easy guide for interviewing and vetting your dude once you get a list of suggestions from friends, family, colleagues, neighbors, etc.

Let's start the vetting process with the easiest pass/fail test ever: did the dude call you back? If the dude is hard to reach as you're actively trying to give him your money, how well do you think he'll respond when he already has your money? Bad communication is NOT A THING.

If he calls back, and you schedule a meeting, get ready for the next test: did you get any creep factor from the visit? This is critical—if you are for any reason uncomfortable with the actions or language of the dude, say thanks but no thanks. Trusting your gut is a THING.

Next test: since you're so well prepared for the visit and will have the contents of your BRAIN handy, is dude actively listening to your needs and desires (and giving you mad props for being awesomely involved)? If you're being talked *at* instead of listened *to*, it's time to move on down the list of referrals.

did dude *call* you back?

did you get a *good feeling* or the *creeps?*

did dude *actively listen?*

So far so good? Let's start seriously checking out the dude to make sure that he knows his stuff and is able to keep you safe as he does it.

• licensing: each state has a licensing agency that is searchable online for the current status of all builders. You want a licensed builder so that he is educated about all the local building codes (many states require 60+ hours of education and a thorough exam) and is able to pull all necessary building permits for proper inspections. You can request a copy of dude's license number issued by the state and search for any previous violations, sanctions and current status.

• referrals: Listen up please: I don't care if your mother-in-law swears up and down that the nice fellow she heard about on Facebook is THE ONE and should be hired on the spot. You MUST ask dude for referrals and check up on each one.

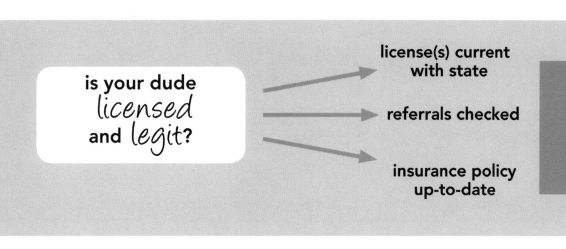

is your dude *licensed* and *legit*?

→ license(s) current with state

→ referrals checked

→ insurance policy up-to-date

keep going!

• insurance: your dude should have a current liability insurance policy for the minimum amount required by each state. It's best if the coverage is one million dollars with additional operations coverage in order to protect both his workers and your home. Ask for a copy of the insurance policy and feel free to call the insurance agent listed to confirm that the policy is current and not lapsed. You can also request from the contractor to have your name placed temporarily on that policy to be notified immediately if there is a lapse in coverage.

Next big question: who's the boss? Tony Danza certainly won't be running your job, so find out who will be. Often the slick, logo-emblazened-oxford-wearin'-big-truck-drivin'-well-mannered dude who showed up when you called is NOT the one who will be project managing or completing the physical work. Find out who will be doing those two things and request to meet the person responsible for overseeing the job. The creep factor rule applies to this dude as well.

who's the *boss*?

Project Manager

Alyssa Milano?

are the subs *dependable & reliable*?

Home stretch: your last concern before signing on the dotted line is asking about the subcontractors. A general contractor will not possess all trade skills, so he'll "sub out" many bits of the job (plumbing, electrical, hvac) to other licensed professionals. Ask about which subcontractors will be used on your project and how long the dude has been working with them. You have a right to know who will have access to your home during the project, so you need to feel comfortable with those folks as well. If you have any concerns about the GC/sub relationship, call the office of the subcontractor and ask about how long they've worked together. "Would you hire XYZ Contracting for your own remodel?" is a valid (and revealing) question to ask the subs.

Winner winner chicken dinner! You made it through the flow chart of "dude-choosing" and are ready to partner up with your successfully vetted dude to tackle your remodel! Before you sign on the dotted line, let's take a look at what comes before that signature page on the contract to ensure that you and your dude have the same expectations for the remodel.

winner!

winner, winner chicken dinner!

Bidness

As you're choosing your dude, keep in mind that serious contractors who have an established reputation like to set their "bidness" apart from their competition. Let's investigate the most frequently used pitch lines by contractors during first meetings with potential clients and uncover the true meanings behind them:

"I'm the best known company in town. My name is everywhere!": this is a sign that their advertising budget is so large that they need to hustle to cover next month's radio ad fee. If you're paying for a name, it's likely that the General Contractor (GC) subcontracts all the work, often to other contractors, who don't need to advertise because they're getting work from the Big Name guy. If you can find out who the subcontracted contractor is and hire them as the GC instead, that could save some money and make the line of communication one branch shorter.

"My work is the best quality you'll ever find!": if the contractor likes himself a little too much, you might find yourself in a situation where he wants control of the overall design and will change details based on his own opinion rather than your direct wishes. If he's just trying to add your project to his portfolio instead of ensuring that you get the remodel you've been dreaming of, you might not get the results you expect.

"Oh, you got a bid from XYZ Contracting? They're hacks!": disparaging another company is never cool. It takes the focus off the quality and integrity of the contracting company you're interviewing. Within the industry, it's considered a pretty douchey move to smack talk competitors.

"If you sign the contract right now, I'll give you $1000 off!": walk away. There should never be any pressure to have you sign a contract, especially if signing immediately prevents you from doing reference checks and taking time to THINK about the contract.

While the physical "bidness" of remodeling needs to be executed by a licensed contractor, it is up to you how many other home improvement professionals are involved in your project. There are some architects and interior designers who will project manage and oversee the entire process if you desire. I'm personally a huge fan of ringleading jobs for my clients so I can control the quality of their remodel experience. The most important aspect for you to consider for project management is this: if the shit hits the fan at 10pm on a Sunday, who do you trust to answer your phone call?

Trust your gut!
Research the crap out of any home improvement professional and feel comfortable with the role they'll play in your remodel. Don't hand over your keys and cash to a dude until you find one you like and trust without hesitation.

It is in your best interest to thoroughly research any contractor. Look online at your state's licensing and regulatory agency to ensure that the contractor is licensed in your state and able to pull the necessary permits to keep your home safe. You'll also want a copy of their current insurance policy, which they will gladly provide to prove that they're legit.

CONTRACTY BITS

When it comes to reviewing your remodel contract (and you WILL review it in significant detail, because you are a GOOD and CAUTIOUS client), I want you to look at it with two goals in mind: first,

> I once had a contractor write out a "contract" in chicken scratch for my bathroom remodel on a coffee-stained yellow legal pad. I declined the job and hired the oxford-wearin'-big-truck-drivin' dude instead. Professionalism is a THING.

ensuring that the document looks legit and that the pricing, terms and specifications will protect you and your family. Do not be bashful about asking for clarification or changes to the contract (because you, like Tony Danza, are the boss). Second (and most critically): ensure that all the hard work and effort you and your spouse put into planning exercises for this remodel located in the BRAIN are clearly represented in this legal document. Once signed, this contract will be an

unstoppable force that will eat up considerable amounts of your money, time and energy. Take time now to analyze and go through each line item to make damn sure it aligns with your BRAIN goals.

Contract Must-Haves

Services CONTRACT

• Scope of work and time frame clearly indicated

• Thorough listing of deliverables
(drawings, presentations, samples)

• Cost, whether flat rate or hourly or % of contract,
and payment structure

Construction CONTRACT

• Scope of work and time frame clearly indicated

• Itemized and thorough listing of
labor and materials

• Reasonable amounts for budgeted allowances

• Payment structure clearly defined

• Change order policy & fees explained

• Listing of exclusions, if any

do:
ballsy lists

PROACTIVE COMMUNICATION

Being picky about the selection of your dude and having a solid contract in hand are just a few pieces of the puzzle when it comes to the overall success of your remodel project. Having the balls and forethought to talk openly about your expectations for behavior and performance for the remodel with your contractor, family, kids and other key players impacted by the project is the most critical key to overall success. These folks can't read your mind, so specific requests will need to be made crystal clear from the onset. Trust me—it's far more awkward in the middle of the project to confront the Project Manager with the feedback of "I don't want those men pooping in my downstairs half bath" than it is to establish up front that a Porta Potty would be your preference.

Making the lists and having those conversations up front will make your remodel a much more enjoyable experience.

"I don't want those men pooping in my downstairs half bath."

Proactive Communicating Tips

Kids

"No, Timmy, the contractor's framing nailer does NOT SHOOT NERF BULLETS. Put it down, sweetie, so you don't kill your sister." Be clear with your kids about never touching the tools on the job site, and make sure the contractors know there are curious tots underfoot.

Boss

Tell your boss if you're remodeling since you'll likely use some time during working hours to deal with meetings, walk-throughs or issues that arise during construction. Be clear with the contractor about acceptable means of communication during working hours.

Family

The worst time to think about an emergency plan is *during an emergency*. Make a plan before remodeling starts for a proper escape route if there is a fire and regular exits will be blocked by construction. Consider an alternate shelter location for tornadoes or storms if your usual spot is compromised.

Contractor

Set ground rules for job site expectations that the contractor and subs should follow. Address cleanliness, safety, language, radio stations, dress code, and bathroom usage. Be painfully honest up front to avoid uncomfortable conversations down the road.

Construction Considerations

By this point, you've worked hard to get your remodeling plan in place using the worksheets and activities from both the communication and cash sections of Remodeling Your House without Killing Your Spouse. You've also assembled a team of trustworthy home improvement professionals to execute your awesome design. Before work begins in earnest, it's important to examine a few more ways that you and your partner can be proactive with your cash: establishing a worst case scenario fund, prioritizing structural vs. aesthetic jobs, preventing overinvestment, and planning for short term/long term projects.

WORST CASE SCENARIO FUND

Superhero contractors who wear red capes and have Xray vision are totally a THING. Unfortunately, most contractors are mere mortals who cannot see what lurks behind the walls and under the floors of your home until they tear into it. The more experienced your contractor, the greater the chance that you'll be forewarned about pricey unexpected structural or code issues that could potentially pop up during your remodel. If the contractor has seen issues in your age or location of home, he should be mentioning that it's possible repairs will need to be made on the fly (and that you'll be billed immediately for them). For this reason, I recommend writing in a line item for my contracts called the WCS: Worst Case

Scenario fund. The line item totals 5% of the overall budget and is used to cover the time and materials cost for any unexpected repairs needed during the remodel. The existence of this fund prevents the "Oh shit, what do we have to cut from the plan now?" moment when you discover that a slow leak has rotted your bathroom floor beyond belief. If you're lucky and there weren't any nasty discoveries during the job, that money is applied to the final payment. It's a win/win, so talk to your contractor about utilizing the WCS fund for your project and set a budget based on the age and condition of your home.

STRUCTURAL VS. AESTHETICS JOBS
STORYTIME: MRS. FLUFFY

A new client in a posh subdivision hired me for a color consultation for her large dining room. As I interviewed Mrs. Fluffy, she explained that she had planned a very large and important dinner party for her husband's colleagues the week before Halloween. "I have to make a perfect impression!" she chanted as I pulled out a few paint swatches. Taping a few colors to the wall, I noticed a wicked leak in the corner that ran down the wall adjacent to the garage. "Oh, did you have a good experience with your roofing contractor to fix this leak?" I asked. The client stared at me for a moment, then stopped petting the white fluffy designer dog in her hands. "My roofie what?" she asked, tilting her head. "Roofing contractor," I replied. "For the repair." Still nothing. "For THIS leak," I said, pointing at the brown stain in the corner.

"Ohhhhhh, that thing. Aren't you just going to....." She made magic waving motions with her hands, jostling the fluffy creature. "tooooo......paint over it?" she finished, making kissing noises at the dog.

I explained to Mrs. Fluffy that before the drywall could be patched and repaired, the roof leak needed to be addressed. "Structure before aesthetics," I said. She tilted her very pretty head, then said "but my dinner party is in 5 days. Can't you just paint over it now and I'll get those roofie people out to fix the thingy in the spring?" I began to explain once again about structural issues, then stopped myself when I recalled that Mrs. Fluffy's husband was a cardiologist. "Let me put it this way: if your husband had a patient who needed bypass surgery, would he first suggest that the patient have his teeth whitened?" She considered the analogy for a moment, then addressed the fluffy creature. "Daddy wouldn't like that one bit, would he Love?" Turning her attention to me, she sighed, then asked me to arrange for the "roofie people" to come quickly to fix the issue.

Maintaining the structural integrity of your home trumps any aesthetic jobs. It sucks to put a ton of money into work that you don't really see, but the benefit is living in a home that won't, ya know, fall down. Safety is a THING. Talk to your dude about any maintenance work that will need to be addressed before the remodel begins.

remodeling your house without killing your spouse

OVERINVESTING
STORYTIME: FRANKENBATH

I met my client Frank many years ago when he hired me to design a kick-ass bathroom for his very modest home. When I first interviewed Frank and heard his lengthy list of non-negotiables for the remodel, I flinched.

I carefully looked around the tiny house and peered out the window towards the other incredibly small homes in that neighborhood. "Frank," I began, "you're about to spend a great deal of money on this bathroom. Remodeling to this extent will over-improve your home so much that you'll price yourself out the market if you ever want to sell."

"Oh, I'm completely aware of that!" he replied. He explained that he grew up in that home and his mother had recently passed, leaving both the home and some cash to him. "I never intend to move. Too many memories here," he said. "So let's do this."

I collaborated with Frank to create a spa-like bathroom with amazing custom details that ended up totaling more than the pre-remodel value of his home. Was he thrilled? Absolutely. Do I recommend this for everyone? No. If you intend to sell your home within 10 years of remodeling, consult a realtor for advice about comparable homes in your neighborhood to determine what's reasonable and justifiable for resale purposes.

SHORT TERM VS. LONG TERM
STORYTIME: DEMANDASAURUS REX

"Demandasaurus Rex" is the kindest description I can offer for my client Veruca. She and her husband Mr. Salt were interested in a major remodel for their open kitchen and living room, but Mr. Salt was only willing to pony up for the kitchen remodel since he had recently purchased pricey new living room furniture for Veruca the previous year. "But I want it NOW!" she told her husband during the consultation. "I'll get it for you, sweetheart, but let's wait just a little longer and..."

"NOW" Veruca refrained. "Well, honey, see, I'll get my bonus in a few months and we'll use that money to...." "I WANT IT NOW!!" she yelled, jumping up from the table and stomping her feet as she left the room in a huff.

I looked at Mr. Salt, who offered me a weak smile and a quick apology. "She's just....." "Going to break out in song? Because I'd pay to see that." I told him.

I explained to Mr. Salt that I understood Veruca's wishes to do both projects simultaneously. "It's a bad bit of remodeler's remorse when you're sitting in one perfect space and have to look at the not-so-perfect adjoining space" I explained. "So I have a suggestion if you and your wife are willing to hear me out." I offered to design both a short term and long term plan for their room. The short term details included the full kitchen remodel that they could implement immediately, and the long term plan showed all of the elements of the living room updates. The bonus and beautiful compromise of the short term plan, however, was in utilizing 10% of the overall kitchen budget that Mr. Salt had originally approved and implementing phase 1 of the living room. While Veruca did have to wait several months for the full living room upgrade, she was able to get all new flooring in both rooms at the time of the kitchen remodel. Mr. Salt was thrilled with the compromise. Veruca stopped stomping for a few minutes, so I considered it a success.

If your remodel project adjoins another space that also needs an update, ask your designer for plans to address that area, both short-term and long-term using a small percentage of the overall budget.

YOUR TURN

The lessons of the worst case scenario fund, Mrs. Fluffy's roof leak, the Frankenbath and Veruca's "I want it NOW" attitude all help explain the importance of being proactive with your cash. Analyzing your remodeling projects and determining what needs to be addressed first is the most prudent course of action, so talk with your spouse and contractor about these four proactive cash issues to get the most out of your remodel.

Don't Be a Dick

I want to wrap up the cash section with a final note of consideration for the relationships you develop with your home improvement professionals. I'll be as blunt as possible about this topic, because it always kills me when there's an altercation during a project. Here's a fact that I want you to be prepared for despite the best planning: shit WILL go wrong during construction. Items will be backordered, subcontractors will fall behind because of schedule conflicts, and materials will arrive damaged. I've seen every precaution taken, and yet something will still go wrong. It just does.

Here's the thing, though: when it hits the fan, please DO NOT attack the individuals who have the power to fix things for you. We understand that you're upset, but screaming at or belittling your home improvement professional will only inflame the situation when all we're trying to do it fix things for you as quickly as possible.

...shit WILL go wrong during construction...

If whatever went wrong is truly a mistake (and 99% of the time, it is—contract work runs on too thin of a margin for workers to be able to screw things up without losing a ton of money) instead of a flagrant, willful deed, then here is the recommended course of action:

remodeling your house without killing your spouse

1. If your dude doesn't already know of the issue, inform him immediately.

2. Ask why it happened along with how it can be prevented in the future.

3. Ask for the dude's plan and timeline to fix the situation.

4. Ask dude to follow up with you when the fix is both underway and completed.

I guarantee that your problem will be solved faster and more willingly by your dude if you approach the situation with civility instead of hostility. I'm not saying that you have to remove all emotion from the situation; it's completely understandable that you're going to be upset when something goes wrong. Just please, please don't be a dick to the people who have the power to solve your problem.

The use of the phrase *'you people'* is one of the most offensive things you can say to home improvement professionals as it implies that the referenced group is less important than normal humans. Insults are NOT A THING.

remodeling your house without killing your spouse

Cash Hall of Fame

Blingy PETS

Many clients spend crap-tons of cash on their beloved pets. I once had clients whose cat was so revered that they asked me to modify custom cabinetry in their master bathoom in order to house the litterbox. "Mr. Sniggles doesn't like the basement litterbox, does he my little snuggle wuggums mwah mwah mwahhh" Mrs. Felinatrix gushed to her standoff-ish cat as she forced kisses on his ear-flattened head. Since I couldn't interview the primary user of the space (I tried, but Mr. Sniggles simply licked his butt in re-sponse), I relied on my client to provide the functional and aesthetic information I would need to complete the design. A month later, Mr. Sniggles had a completely pimped-out, private, functional litterbox with a $3000 price tag that made his human very happy.

Cash Hall of Fame

To GO

"We want the best of everything!" was the direction given by the Flashington couple on their kitchen remodel. "A Wolf 6 burner stove, granite countertops, custom cabinetry—everything in this magazine picture. THIS picture," Mrs. Flashington pointed menacingly with her immaculately manicured index finger. "Certainly, but could you first please tell me about who cooks and how you'll use the kitchen on a daily basis?" The Flashingtons looked at each other, then back at me. "Just give me this picture," the wife said. "But add one thing: a bookcase here where I can store the binder with all the takeout menus." Mr. Flashington nodded, then stated "We don't cook. We're just doing this for resale."

I looked carefully at the couple. "Soooo your budget is $75,000 for a shelf that holds your takeout menus?" I asked, puzzled. "Yup," they said.

TAKE-OUT MENU

Collaborate and Listen

Stop for a hot minute and think very hard about how you and your spouse deal with money. Financial hardship is one of the top cited reasons for divorce in the United States, so don't screw around with this topic and expect to make it out unscathed if you're not willing to talk openly about the impact this kind of expenditure will have on your relationship. If you have ANY hesitation about continuing the process, then have a frank conversation with your partner about your specific concerns and decide how you want to proceed.

I'll give the same warning now as I did at the wrap-up of the communication chapter: the WORST thing you could do right now is plow ahead and ignore any red flags from your partner. Refusing to work together to establish budgets and discuss priorities for the project is a big indicator that your partner just isn't up for remodeling. At this point, you're engaged, but haven't walked down the aisle and said "I do" to remodeling yet. You can back out now and prevent heartache if you know that a project this size just isn't part of your future.

Cash Up, Wrap Up

Congratulations on completing the second section of Remodeling Your House without Killing Your Spouse! Before we move on to the awesomeness of the CRAP language, let's get our poop in a group and review the contents of your BRAIN. I'll sing "She Works Hard for the Money" by Donna Summer while you go gather all the goods. Ready?

At this point, your BRAIN binder should be in a central location with divider tabs for the "do" assignments for both spouses. We'll be adding more tabs shortly, but here is what should be completed and stored from the CASH section:

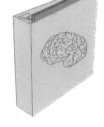

- established budget amount
- priority list
- notes from choosing your dude
- remodeling contract review
- ballsy list of proactive requests
- construction considerations

Remember, all of the forms in the book can be accessed on the Remodeling Your House without Killing Your Spouse website: www.hddbook.com.

Humor fixes everything. If you're having trouble communicating with your spouse about cash-related topics for your remodel, whip out a good joke to lighten the mood. Here's a little story just to give you an idea of the depth of humor in my family: When my music-loving mama died unexpectedly, I created a playlist using CDs from her car for the funeral visitation. Imagine the looks on the guests' faces when they heard the Kelis lyrics "my milkshake brings all the boys to the yard" playing softly. Humor is a THING.

To some owners, a home is just a financial investment where you put your stuff to get a legit billing address. To others, a home is a marker of identity and responsibility of stewardship that lasts for generations. Most folks fall in the middle of that spectrum, so consider how emotionally attached you are to your home before you decide what you're willing to invest in remodeling.

Brand Whore
[brand] [hawr, hohr
or, often, hoor], noun

A person who insists upon purchasing popular brand name items at a higher cost than comparable items for the purpose of tooting one's own horn or rubbing it in the faces of the neighbors (despite the fact that many economical alternatives exist and would be a better fit for their budget).

You know you're ready to move on when......

You've completed this group of assignments and have consensus for the scope of the project and who will be completing it. More specifically, moving on to the CRAP section requires meaningful and productive conversations with your spouse about the following key concepts:

- establishing a reasonable remodel budget
- respecting your partner's priority list
- addressing the reality checks
- hiring a non-creepy, totally vetted dude (or team)
- communicating proactively with your dude
- being proactive with your money
- assembling the BRAIN with completed worksheets

c.r.a.p

do

> "It's always a more valid argument to say "The color contrast of the kitchen cabinets with the granite countertop is too visually jarring." rather than "Ick. That sucks donkey balls and I don't like it." See? Language is power."

learn

enjoy

C.R.A.P.

Robin Williams is a genius. No, not the comedy God (though I still quote The World According to Garp with reverence); I mean the digital design Goddess who wrote the best-selling Non-Designer's Design Book. I found a copy of this book accidentally one day as I waited in my husband's MSU campus office for our lunch date. I had just come from a client consultation where I had applied good design principles to help reorganize and decorate her space and tried unsuccessfully to teach the key concepts so she could apply those ideas to the next room. "What was that grouping thing you talked about again?" she asked. I tried to explain balance and form to her, but the idea was too abstract for her to fully embrace.

So as my tummy rumbled, I started looking through the shelves of my husband's office and came across the name Robin Williams. Muttering "....but to have it bitten off in a Buick...," I flipped through the pages of the Non-Designer's Design Book. I quickly realized that though this book was intended for two-dimensional website design practices, all of the key concepts were completely transferrable to three-dimensional design as well. Bonus: it had a name that would be easily teachable to clients. Double bonus: its name was CRAP!

> If you've ever walked into a space and said "Something's off. I just don't like it," the CRAP was out of balance.

CRAP is an acronym for four key design elements: Contrast, Repetition, Alignment and Proximity. It is the presence and balance of these four elements that allows you to feel harmony, happiness and contentment in a space. Think of it as a more sciency version of feng shui and you get the idea.

Happiness and contentment, however, are relative. In the same way that people have unique tolerances for spicy food or loud music, everyone has differing levels of preference for each element in the CRAP scale. Let's take a look at the CRAP scale and talk about our Goldilocksian feelings for a hot minute to determine where you and your partner fall on the CRAP scale.

meh....   *juuuuuuuust right!*   *FREAK OUT!!!*

Where do you fall on the c.r.a.p. scale?

meh....

FREAK OUT!!!

If you think beige is a racy color, you'll land here on the scale.

meh....

If you're a six year old boy hopped up on a dozen pixie stix and a large Mountain Dew, you'll land here on the scale.

FREAK OUT!!!

remodeling your house without killing your spouse

If you look at a space and think "OMIGODOMIGOD NO NO NO", you're at the freak-out end of the CRAP scale. If your reaction to that space is "meh……" you're at the bored end of the scale. If you're lucky enough to feel positive emotional response to the space, then guess what?! Your porridge is juuuuuust right (and located in the middle).

Understanding the elements of Contrast, Repetition, Alignment and Proximity will not only allow you to diagnose and treat any imbalance you find in your CRAP scale, but will also allow you to properly communicate and accurately explain your likes and dislikes to your spouse and family. It's always a more valid argument to say "The color contrast of the kitchen cabinets with the granite countertop is too visually jarring." rather than "Ick. That sucks donkey balls and I don't like it." See? Language is power.

The Blandification of America trend of beigifying spaces is creating an over-abundance of snoozefest rooms that are more effective than 4mg of Xanax at removing all feeling.

remodeling your house without killing your spouse

Contrast

Contrast

r

a

p

Contrast highlights differences in elements to show visual interest in a room. Too little contrast is a snoozefest, and too much contrast is visually jarring. There are three ways to achieve contrast in a room: color, texture and size. Let's take a look at how each element impacts the overall look.

"This is so depressing... I have some of the best linework I've ever done and you can hardly see it because I have to paint it black. And beige is its only contrast. Sigh."
– Molly,
RYHWKYS Illustrator

CONTRAST: COLOR

Color is the easiest way to add contrast in this example. Adding dark brown pillows to this neutral sofa in a room with neutral flooring and neutral walls will guarantee that your eye seek out the contrast between the field of the sofa and ground of the pillows. While brown isn't exactly a color, it still achieves contrast (though an actual color appearing in the rainbow would be more effective and pleasant. But I digress.....that's for my next book called Color Coward). So if you're truly a Color Coward, you'll appreciate the next way to achieve contrast in a room: texture.

Dark pillows on a neutral sofa create color contrast.

Ccontrast
r
a
p

CONTRAST: TEXTURE

Texture is more about tactile sense than visual sense, but it plays a key role in the overall room scheme. If the thought of contrasting toss pillows through color gives you hives, try using a textured fabric in the same color saturation. Velvet, corduroy, boucle and sateen are all excellent choices for a tactile experience with toss pillows. Other ways to add texture include throws, rugs, wall coverings, window treatments and twiggy floral arrangements.

A textured throw provides tactile contrast in this arrangement.

CONTRAST: SIZE

Size matters. (Yes, I went there). The scale of furnishings in your room should flow nicely and fit comfortably not only from piece to piece, but also within the room. Don't make the mistake of putting a diminutive antique coffee table in front of GARGAN-TUAN SOFA. The contrast of mismatched size pieces is overwhelming.

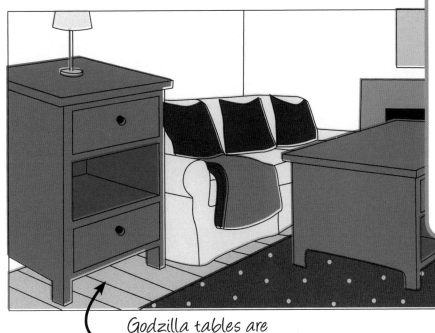

Godzilla tables are
NOT a thing!

Sectionals are evil. They look deceptively cute and compact in a 100,000sq ft furniture showroom, but they look more 'roided up than Mark McGwire when you get them in your room. Don't furniture shop without measuring your space first and setting firm limits on the size.

remodeling your house without killing your spouse

repetition

Repetition

Repetition asserts a theme through multiples. "Theme" can be interpreted in many ways: a style, a genre, a look—it doesn't matter what you call it; your eye will search for common elements within the room and try to make sense of the story you're trying to tell.

70/30 RULE

Let me be completely clear to those of you who are strict interpreters: themes are for parties, not for rooms. I'll make this easy for you by turning it into a math example. You'll always have great thematic balance of repetition as long as you don't violate the 70/30 rule. If more than 70% of the elements in a room (architecture, accessories, furnishings, drapery, wallcovering, etc) are thematically linked, you will feel like you're being beaten over the head by that theme. BUT, if less than 30% of the elements are thematically linked, you won't know what the hell is going on in the room (much like watching any season finale directed by Alan Ball). Stick to the middle when it comes to themes and you'll have a better balance of repetition in the area.

REPETITION: 70% RULE

Our Love Boat example is more than 70% flooded with nautical goodness. Ladies and children first to the life boats, please.
Do you have the theme from The Love Boat in your head yet? Ahoy

matey! Thar she blows! Shiver me timbers! Those references are getting old, right? Would you like me to stop? How many gold doubloons will you pay me to stop? A treasure chest full, perhaps?

I just did with the written word what this room example does with an overbearing, obnoxious theme: I went overboard (snort). Don't take your thematic décor too far—it makes guests shake their heads and talk smack about your décor behind your back. "That poor thing," they'll say. "She just didn't know when to stop."

c
r repetition
a
p

Let's visit the flip side of over-theming: under-theming. This less-than-thirty-percent-land is the equivalent of walking through a modern art museum and trying to make sense of the installation with a single banana peel on a pedestal. Everybody around you is TRYING to make sense of it, and you might overhear a pretentious hipster discuss the nominalization of the fruit workers as an interpretation of the display, but it's still just a fucking banana on a pedestal.

Don't make people guess what your intentions are with the décor. A single conch shell on a coffee table DOES NOT MAKE A NAUTICAL THEME. Dig deeper and find elements to connect the theme using color, texture and size.

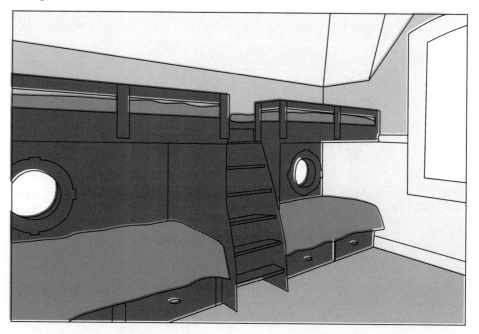

remodeling your house without killing your spouse

REPETITION: QUANTITY

Repetition of quantity is another way that CRAP can be out of balance in a room and is often evident in displays of collectibles.

All of us are accidental collectors in some way. Whether we genuinely intended to amass a collection of certain things over the years or whether the collection was forced upon us, we must deal with the aftermath.

I've seen my clients deal with accidental collections in many ways: buying new furniture or shelving for growing the display, segregating and relocating the collections, giving everything to a relative or friend, or stashing it in storage.

Some collections come to us either slowly through gifting, or all at once when inherited. There can be considerable emotional attachment to collections, so think through what feelings you're assigning to tangible possessions before making any decisions.

c
r repetition
a
p

As a society, we generally think nothing of breaking out all of our well-preserved and carefully packed Christmas/holiday decorations each year for a total of 4ish weeks, then packing them back up in January. Tree ornaments are important in this ritual: we remove them one by one, reminiscing about the origin of each. "Oh! Little Jimmy made this 15 years ago in grade school when he used to eat paste!" "Wow, honey, remember that trip to Vegas? No? Don't want to talk...about...okay" "Yay! Our honeymoon ornament! Dear, remember when you used to take me OUT TO DINNER EVERY ONCE IN A FREAKIN' WHILE? HUH?"

When the holiday is over, we gladly stash the ornaments and the tree so we can put the sofa back where it belongs and vacuum up the eleventy billion needles embedded in the floor covering.

My point is that we're cool with part-time décor for holiday stuff, so why can't we be cool with part-time décor for collections? If you have too big of a collection, consider these tactics for thinning the herd:

• make a few groupings of the collection that tell a story. Pack up the others and rotate the display seasonally like an art collection (but not as sparsely as the banana on a pedestal. Don't make people guess).

• display parts of the collection in different rooms. This will tie a theme throughout the house, creating more balance through repetition.

• donate some of the display if you've fallen out of love. If you're not sure you can live without the pieces, box them up and put them in a closet for a month. If you can't stand being without them, put them back on display. If you totally forgot they were in there and come across them later, it's time to donate.

c
r
a alignment
p

Alignment

Alignment shows hierarchy through placement. Much like pack law, some things are just more important than others. Your eye is constantly seeking the alpha element in the room and you will feel uncomfortable if that heirarchy isn't identifiable.

There are two critical fails I see often in alignment for both vertical and horizontal planes: horizon décor and perimeter décor. I'll apologize in advance, as I'm about to poke fun at men, the state of Indiana, and punk bands as I explain the concepts.

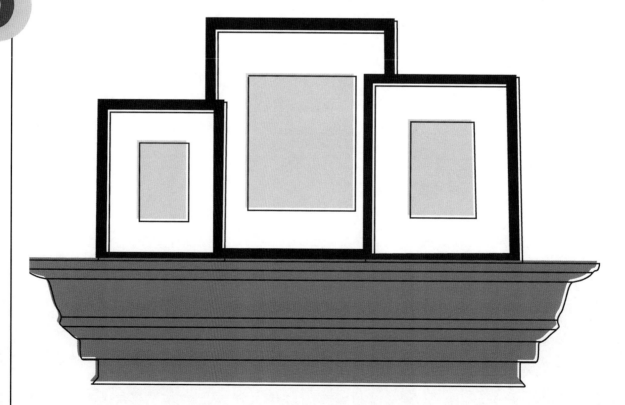

remodeling your house without killing your spouse

ALIGNMENT: HORIZON DECOR

We'll start by discussing art on the wall. There's a definite art to hanging art, and everyone has very strong opinions on the matter. Having seen eleventy billion ways to hang art over the last decade, I'm going to point out the worst extremes that cause CRAP imbalance for alignment.

I generally blame men for what I call "the Indiana effect" in picture hanging. If I walk into a home and see every piece of art hung at exactly the same height alllllll the way around the room, it's a fair bet that Mr. Consistency only wanted to measure ONCE, THANK YOU VERY MUCH, during the hang-fest. What this does to the always-alpha-searching eye, however, is leave it traveling the same height around and around with nothing interesting to focus on, much like driving through long stretches of Indiana highway (I claim rights for poking fun at the Hoosier terrain, as I lived in Lafayette and worked in Indy for many years).

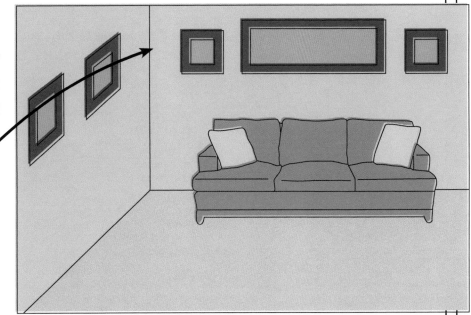

Flatty McFlatterson's eyes will roam with nowhere to land with this "Indiana effect."

c
r
alignment
p

The seasick effect is the opposite of the Indiana effect and results from too many alpha elements on the wall. Your eye bobs up and down faster than a Royal Caribbean boat in a hurricane, resulting in seasickness and general unease. The goal with alignment of art is to encourage your eye to stop and appreciate an element before moving on. When done intentionally, you can force the eye to find the alpha element, then move gracefully around the room on a journey more interesting than Indiana highways and less chaotic than a hurricane cruise.

Bobby McBobberson's eyes will never rest, thanks to this "sea-sick" effect.

Hanging Stuff

When it comes to hanging artwork and other décor, you have three choices: ook, anchor or screw. I promise that's not the name of an indie punk band—it's the list of fasteners available to safely hang your stuff.

Ook

Ook is a brand name of picture hanger that is heads and tails above all basic J style hangers.

- perfect for plaster or drywall usage
- thin guided nail won't harm walls or leave giant holes
- weight rated for 5lbs-100lbs

Anchor

An anchor is used for stability when a stud isn't available.

- select style based on weight requirements
- make pilot hole and insert

Screw

Screws are used to go directly into a stud.

- perform T pin test: big resistance = stud!
- select wood screw based on weight requirements
- make pilot hole and insert

Cheap plastic drywall anchors suck donkey balls. Ditch them in favor of a stronger substitute.

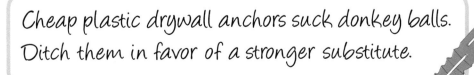

remodeling your house without killing your spouse

HOW TO HANG STUFF

Arranging stuff on the wall is an art form. I could easily spend 100 pages on tips and tricks and top ideas, and you still might not get a good idea. My suggestion is to make a THING section of Pinterest or other magazine & website art arrangement ideas until you find a grouping that feels right for your space.

Hanging stuff, however, is a science. There are tools and math and happiness involved. Remember to use the hardware described in the "Ook, anchor, screw" section for best results. Here are my favorite designer tricks for easy hanging to prevent Indiana-ing and seasickness:

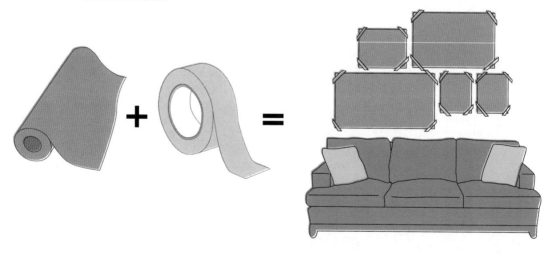

Craft paper and blue painter's tape are a great way to test-drive your arrangement and prevent unnecessary holes in your wall. Measure the sizes of your framed pieces and cut them out of craft paper. Tape the paper to the wall in a few configurations until you're happy with the spacing.

When you're ready to hang your arrangment, use this cool method to measure twice and pound once (all hail Norm Abram):

If your art piece features a wire hanger, grab a metal tape measure and set the art piece on the floor or table with the back facing you. Place the metal tab of the measuring tape on the wire and pull up until the wire is taut. Check the measurement at the top of the frame. This is the distance down from the top of the craft paper that you'll mark on the wall for your nail or other hanging hardware bit.

Float•ing Tang
[floh-ting] [tang], noun
The term for the metal tab on the end of a measuring tape.

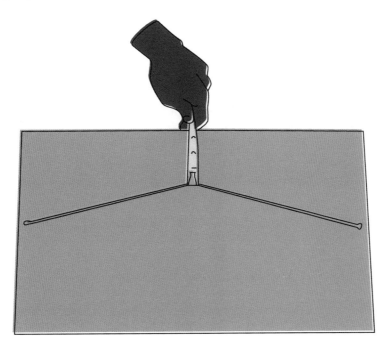

remodeling your house without killing your spouse

c
r
a alignment
p

Now that we've covered vertical spaces with alignment, it's time to look at horizontal configurations. That's right: it's FURNITURE TIME!

In my decade of in-home design consultation experience, I can tell you that people do some silly things with furniture configurations. I've seen it all: lawn chairs, bean bags, futons, crates, cheap stuff, expensive stuff, stuff you're not allowed to sit on, stuff you'll never get up from.....you get the idea. Most of those pieces were configured at right angles and smooshed as close as possible against the perimeter of the room. People love right angles because 90 degree symmetry is a default setting that requires no thought for placement. There's a term I use for the folks with that decor: wall huggers.

If you look at this example, you'll see a traditional furniture selection arranged with militaristic precision against every wall. Not a lot of creativity, but you'll win points with your OCD friends.

I once asked a client why she chose to place her sofa on the longest wall closest to the front door. "Well, that's where the movers left it." she replied. "And Frank has a hernia, sooo.....yeah."

remodeling your house without killing your spouse

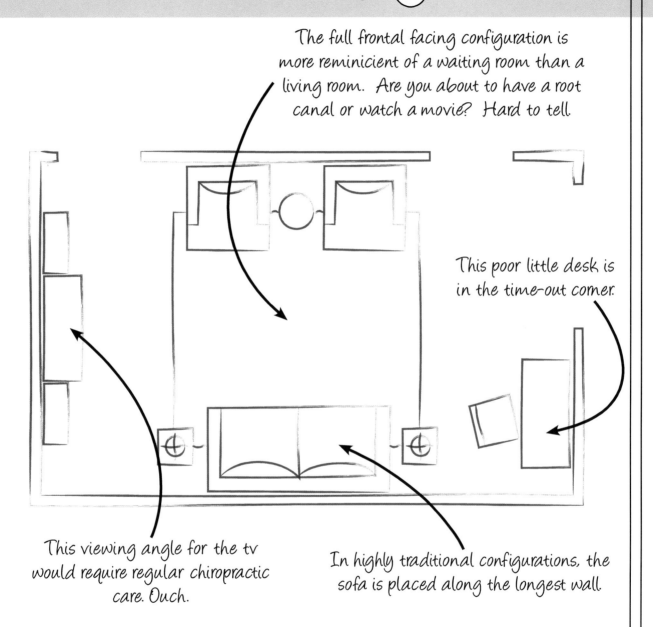

The full frontal facing configuration is more reminicient of a waiting room than a living room. Are you about to have a root canal or watch a movie? Hard to tell.

This poor little desk is in the time-out corner.

This viewing angle for the tv would require regular chiropractic care. Ouch.

In highly traditional configurations, the sofa is placed along the longest wall.

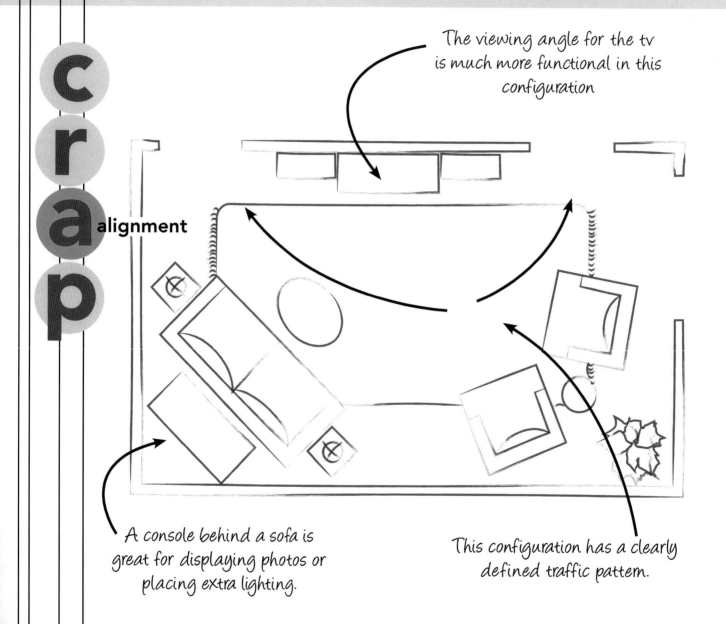

The viewing angle for the tv is much more functional in this configuration

c r a p alignment

A console behind a sofa is great for displaying photos or placing extra lighting.

This configuration has a clearly defined traffic pattern.

If you're willing to contemplate furniture placement options, try playing with angles other than 90 degrees. The only important rules for furniture placement are functional in nature: make sure that there are safe exits and pathways through the room, and be certain that the room still works for you.

Rearranging is a no-cost way to enhance you room, so give it a try. Be safe while moving your pieces, though, and follow these important rules:

- get a non-herniad helper
- wear sturdy shoes
- clear the path
- use the slider thingamabobs for heavy stuff

If you really want to know what your furniture configuration possibilities are, throw a party. Guests won't hesitate to move your furniture to create new conversation groupings or have a better view of the big game on tv. An abundance of adult beverages tends to enhance the creativity.

Proximity

In the 2D design world, proximity is defined as showing similarity among sets of items through location. In 3D spaces, it's really all about function. Stuff's gotta work, or no amount of pretty will cover up the dysfunction. You can work hard in a room to create the perfect contrast, amazing repetition and the most exquisite alignment you've ever seen. BUT: if your room doesn't function, you have failed. Let's investigate issues of function and usefulness for the home.

proximity

PROXIMITY: FUNCTIONAL WORK TRIANGLE

The most hella-obvious area of function in the home is the kitchen. Function is a measurable element based on the effectiveness of the work triangle. The proximity of the geometric path from refrigerator to sink to stove is a make-or-break element in the kitchen. If any leg is too long, you can dribble, drop and scald yourself by carrying things too far. If a leg is too short, you can bump into any passersby and reenact sitcom-style hilarity that ends with a trip to the emergency room. Injuries are NOT A THING, so here's the rule for kitchen function: each leg should be between 4' and 9' long. The total of all three legs should be between 9' and 27' (though 27' is a stretch).

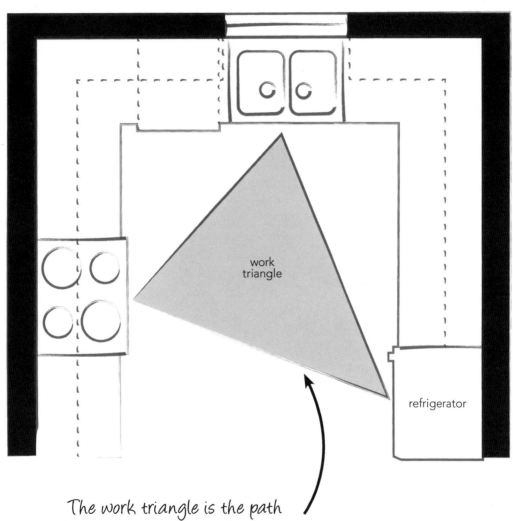

work
triangle

refrigerator

The work triangle is the path
from stove to sink to refrigerator.
U-shaped kitchens often provide
excellent work trianlges.

remodeling your house without killing your spouse

c

r

a

p proximity

Most of my clients stare at floorplans and blueprints with a glazed expression and rely on me to interpret the various lines and symbols. My designer brain has been trained to interpret the 3 dimensional space so I can properly present the information to them. When looking at plans for remodeling, it's important to user-test the virtual space before approving the design. In this example, the entryway is so tight and poorly placed that you would need to stand IN THE OTHER ROOM to open the door wide enough to welcome guests. Single file, right this way.......

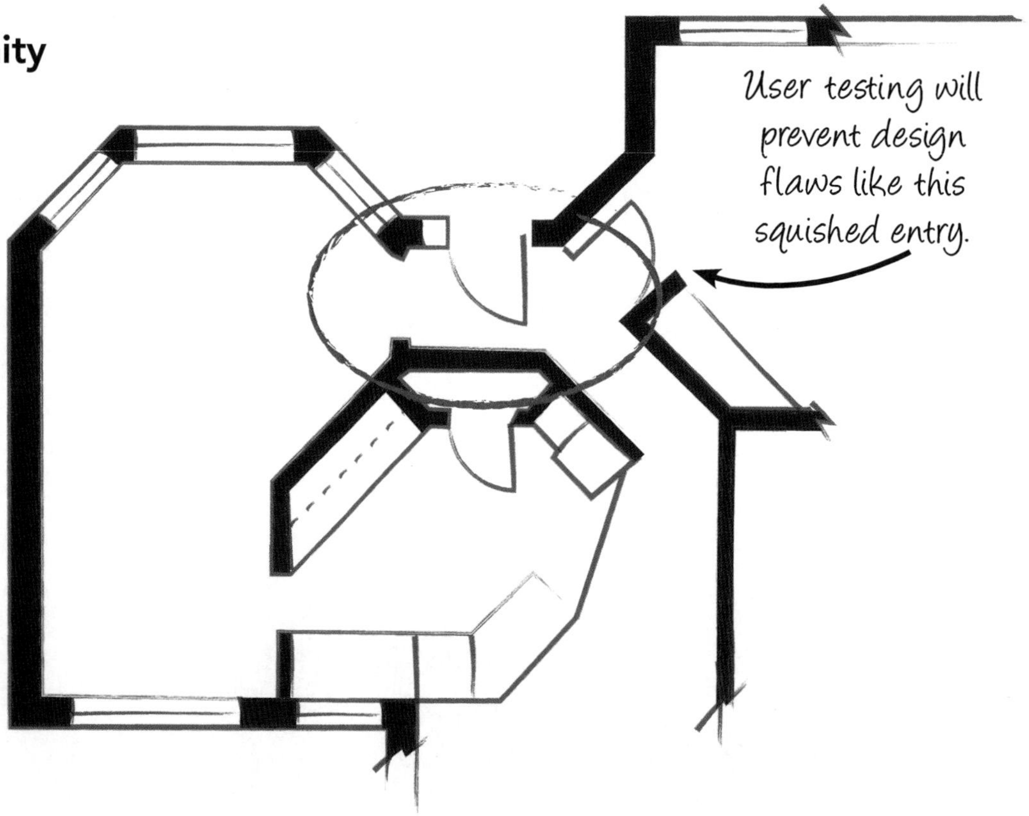

User testing will prevent design flaws like this squished entry.

remodeling your house without killing your spouse

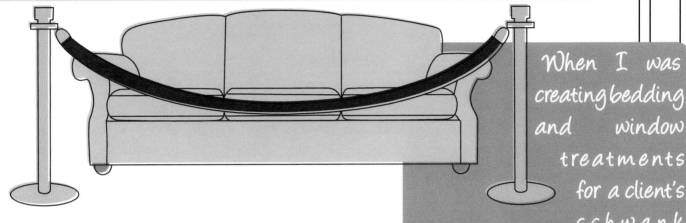

USEFULNESS

Function has a very specific element of usefulness as well that applies to finishes and furnishings in your home. When you were growing up, was there a formal living room in your home that you weren't allowed to enter? Was there a table that was NEVER allowed to have drinks placed on it without a coaster? Any antiques or furniture pieces that were off-limits? Think hard about the usability of furniture when purchasing. If you'll be so worried about your family or guests ruining it that you can't enjoy the piece, it's probably not worth having. Do research on warranties and recommended uses for furniture and finishes before you purchase. Remember: white carpet is NOT A THING.

When I was creating bedding and window treatments for a client's schwank summer home in upstate NY, her young grandchildren arrived to check out the newly constructed home. Stir crazy from a long car ride, the boys decided to run and jump on all the new furniture, including the beds in their room. My client chased the boys around the house with a worried expression, chanting "Grandma loves you... please GET DOWN! Grandma lovDON'T TOUCH THAT!!!"

contrast

repetition

Contrast highlights differences in elements to show visual interest in a room. Too little contrast is a snoozefest, and too much contrast is visually jarring. Finding the balance of this most obvious of the CRAP elements will make a room visually appealing.

Repetition asserts a theme through multiples. "Theme" can be interpreted in many ways: a style, a genre, a look—it doesn't matter what you call it; your eye will search for common elements within the room and try to make sense of the story you're trying to tell.

Three elements in contrast:

- color

- texture

- size

Two elements in repetition:

- theme (70/30 rule)

- quantity
  (accidental collectors)

alignment proximity

Alignment shows hierarchy through placement. Much like pack law, some things are just more important than others. Your eye is constantly seeking the alpha element in the room and will feel uncomfortable if it is unidentifyable.

Proximity is all about function. Stuff's gotta work, or no amount of pretty will cover up the dysfunction. You can achieve the perfect contrast, amazing repetition and the most exquisite alignment you've ever seen. BUT: if your room doesn't function, you have failed.

Two elements in alignment:

- horizon décor (Indiana-ing and seasick)

- perimeter décor (wall huggers and angles)

Two elements in proximity:

- function

- usefulness

do:
treat &
diagnose

R.A.P. in Action

On the FOX drama series, *House MD*, Dr. Gregory House began each medical case with a differential diagnosis that would take into consideration every possible cause for the patient's current symptoms.

Let's use the technique of Dr. House to diagnose and treat a few room scenarios using your new CRAP knowledge. Here are the steps to accomplish CRAP in ACTION:

  1. "Diagnose" the issue by placing yourself on the Goldilocks scale for each element.

  2. Explain your reaction using your new CRAP vocabulary words.

  3. Treat the problem by addressing and correcting the CRAP imbalance.

Holy back in black, Batman! This drawing of a home office features a black desk and hutch, black desk chair, neutral walls and rug, and a series of identically framed black and white family photos.

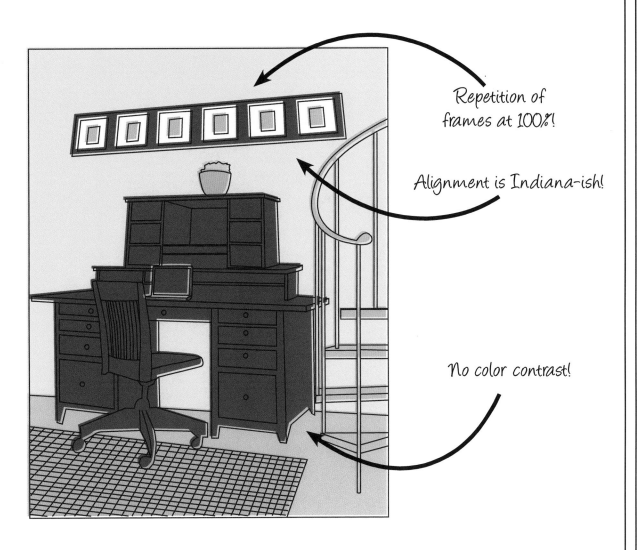

Repetition of frames at 100%!

Alignment is Indiana-ish!

No color contrast!

TREATMENT: CONTRAST

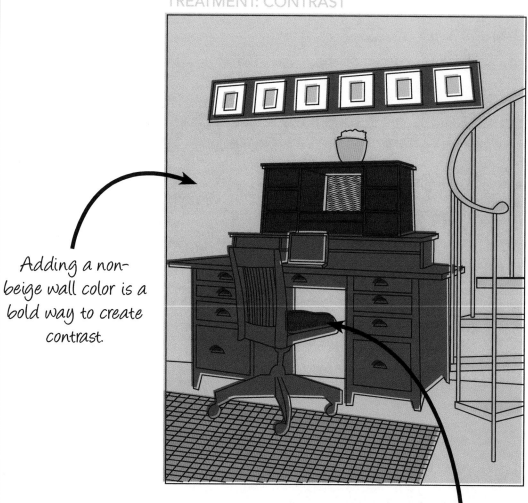

Adding a non-beige wall color is a bold way to create contrast.

If the wall color scares you, try using color on just the hutch or a chair pad. Baby steps are fine!

TREATMENT: REPETITION

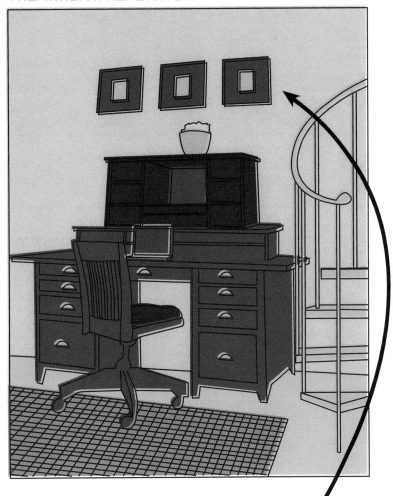

Thinning the herd of family
photos allows the reminaing
pictures to be more meaningful

TREATMENT: ALIGNMENT

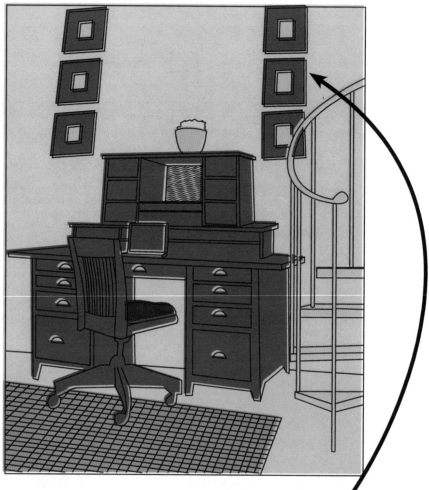

Arrange the photos vertically to highlight the height of the room. The spiral staircase suggests a two-story wall, so taking the eye on a trip up rather than stopping it horizontally is a bonus.

How did you fare with your first differential diagnosis? Were you able to identify the CRAP elements that registered away from your goldilocks location on the CRAP scale? The more you practice, the easier it will be to identify the elements out of balance. Use magazine photos and Pinterest boards for CRAP analysis experience before turning your eye towards your own space.

Shopping in your own home is a great way to create new decor at no cost. Look in other rooms for case pieces and upholstered furniture to help achieve c.r.a.p. balance in your room. The desk shoved in the guest room might fit perfectly in your family room, and the old cedar chest in the bedroom might just make a perfect TV stand.

remodeling your house without killing your spouse

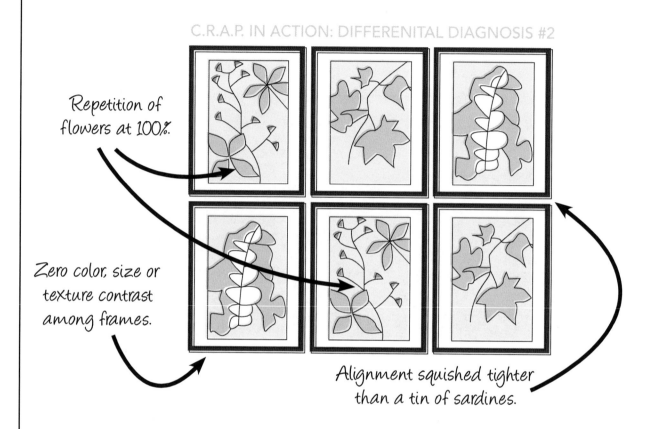

C.R.A.P. IN ACTION: DIFFERENITAL DIAGNOSIS #2

Repetition of flowers at 100%.

Zero color, size or texture contrast among frames.

Alignment squished tighter than a tin of sardines.

The Botanical Field Guide called—they want their reference page back. This drawing of a set of framed and matted botanical art prints was meant to be displayed close together on a large blank wall. The set features identical frames and mats with 3 repeated prints. Ready to put your CRAP language to use? Let's start treatment!

remodeling your house without killing your spouse

TREATMENT: CONTRAST

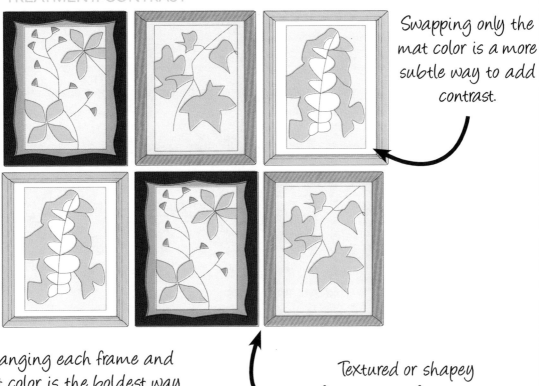

Swapping only the
mat color is a more
subtle way to add
contrast.

Changing each frame and
mat color is the boldest way
to create contrast.

Textured or shapey
frames are a fun way to
achieve contrast.

TREATMENT: REPETITION

 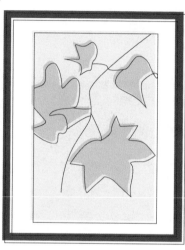 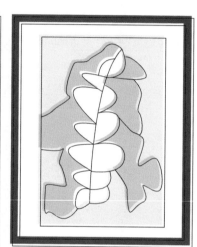

Removing the three identical botantical prints allows the
remaining artwork to be more
prominent and less theme-tastic.

TREATMENT: ALIGNMENT

Enlarging one of the prints creates an alpha element that the eye will gravitate towards.

Arranging the prints non-lineally allows the eye to travel through the grouping.

remodeling your house without killing your spouse

Crap-Up

Empowering my clients to use the CRAP language to communicate effectively with each other is one of the best parts of my job. I feel a sense of pride when the couple can whip out a reference to contrast or repetition when making a statement about a space rather than relying on the standard knee-jerk "this room sucks donkey balls." Being able to communicate with a common CRAP vocabulary accomplishes two important communication goals:

1. It removes subjectivity and creates more equality and merit in the conversation. It's easier to accept the statement "I'd like more contrast in color and texture between the dining table and the floor sample so the table doesn't blend in and look like it's floating in the room." rather than an un-CRAP statement of "if you choose that lame floor tile, I'll shove it up your ass."

During discussions of decor, remember that you know CRAP.

2. It allows a front-row seat for the viewing of your spouse's hidden brain workings. Being able to discuss their reaction to room elements using the scale as a guide with the proper vocabulary to voice what's causing the reaction is liberating. One client told me this after learning CRAP: "We've been married 27 years and I never knew he had a high tolerance for bold color. I would have had red walls twenty years ago if he had just told me!"

Congratulations on completing the third section of Remodeling Your House without Killing Your Spouse! Before we move on to the cool character section, let's get our poop in a group and review the contents of your BRAIN. I'll hum the jeopardy theme while you go gather the goods. Ready?

At this point, your BRAIN binder should be in a central location with divider tabs for the "do" assignments for both spouses. Here is what should be completed and stored from the CRAP section:
- Goldilocks scales for you and your spouse
- differential diagnoses for many Pinterest and magazine rooms

Remember that all of the forms in the book can be accessed through the Remodeling Your House without Killing Your Spouse website: www.hddbook.com. Great room samples for completing your differential CRAP diagnoses can be found on the Hart-Davidson Designs Pinterest site under "designdemocracy".

You know you're ready to move on when......

You've completed this group of assignments and show a command of the CRAP language to effectively communicate with your spouse about the following key concepts:
- diagnosing the CRAP imbalance
- explaining your reaction using CRAP language
- treating the issue to bring the proper balance to your CRAP scale

C.R.A.P. Hall of Fame

Thinning the HERD

The insolent, hilariously smart teenage daughter of a client was punished for a misdeed by dusting all 500 pieces of her mother's Precious Moments figurine colection. "This is a waste of time," Insolent Emma told her mother. "You never even notice them because there are so many." "That's not true! I love them all!" her mother replied.

After The Great Dusting, Insolent Emma tested her theory of how much her mother actually looked at the display by changing the orientation of some of the figurines each day. When her mother bypassed the case of indecently posed figurines for a solid week, Insolent Emma started removing figurines two by two, carefully wrapping them in tissue paper and packing them away with the Christmas ornaments. In total, more than 2/3 of the collection was removed.

It wasn't until a family friend commented on what a lovely and attractive display the figurines made that her mother actually noticed the thinning of the herd. "Why......thank you. My daughter is quite perceptive when it comes to displays." she replied.

Terrifying TAXIDERMY

Moving to Michigan a decade ago, I discovered just how much guys love trophies. I'm not talking about the metal, raise-over-your-head-in-sports kind of trophies. I'm referring to hunting trophies: bigass dead animals. Hunting is a THING in Michigan, so it is quite common to see giant deer mounts used as home décor.

I was designing the small formal living room space for a couple battling over the real estate above their fabulous new stone fireplace. Mr. Taxidermy insisted that his latest massive buck mount would look impressive on the stone fireplace, but Mrs. Hesitant insisted that the dead critter creeped her out. Since my job was to referee and ensure that both of them could equally enjoy the space, I taught them the language of CRAP to better communicate their ideas.

After the lesson, Mrs. Hesitant was able to say this: "Honey, the size contrast of your impressive mount is so overwhelming that it will overshadow the beauty of the natural stone that you selected for the fireplace. Why don't we put that BIG mount in your mancave and you can tag a mount next season that's a better scale for the room?" Mr. Taxidermy gladly agreed, appreciating both the compliment and the green light for more dead critter decor in the house.

character

do

fire test   160

> "Here's the thing: if you could go out and re-purchase every single item in your home right now, then there isn't enough shit you could ever buy to fill the hole in your soul."

learn

enjoy

Blandification

It's no secret that I loathe the color beige. My disdain for the color burns hotter than the light from eleventy billion buring suns. I want to vomit every time I hear the host of a home improvement show say "we'll neutralize all the bold color and paint every wall this classic beige" (and I guarantee that my vomit is more colorful than the wall).

> **Beige** [beyzh], adjective
> 1. A variable color averaging light grayish-yellowish brown
> 2. A pale to grayish yellow
> 3. The bane of Leslie's existence as a designer

A little part of my soul dies every time I see a homeowner choose neutrality over personality for their home. It is a dangerous trend on par with the decade of the Waverly print-on-print-on-print that made your retinas scream "Uncle!" when you walked into the room. The decorative pendulum swings mightily for this trend, so I'd like to explain how it came about and how you can avoid it.

remodeling your house without killing your spouse

Somebody hand me a soapbox, because I intend to rant. Before I begin: if you are a real estate agent, you might want to skip this section. I'm about to blame your profession for a little something that I call THE BLANDIFICATION OF AMERICA.

The housing market bubble that wreaked havoc on builders, home improvement specialists and real estate in general from 2007-2013ish made everyone involved take a hard look at what was necessary to make an existing home attractive to the few qualified buyers available. Real estate themed shows started popping up on all the networks, and agents were dutiful in their task to get the homes sold fast. Their mantra: neutralize the décor to attract as many buyers as possible. Beige became the poster child of the selling game as homeowners raced to remove ANY element from their home that could POSSIBLY offend a potential buyer. As these shows gained popularity, the trend of neutrality took hold. Home décor and furniture suppliers reacted quickly and began stocking their shelves with beigiest of all beige items. Upholstery, lighting, artwork, rugs—all elements became the least offensive, most neutral incarnations possible. Homeowners recognized the trend set forth in the real estate shows and furthered the neutrality agenda by snatching up all of the beigetastic décor available. When I recognized that the neutral décor was spreading like an insidious virus,

> **"And how do we begin to covet, Clarice? We begin by coveting what we see every day"**

I had nightmares of clients ordering up tanker trucks filled with beige paint to hose down every surface in their home (complete with the beep-beep-beep backing up noise). I had to take action to stop The Blandification of America, so let's examine how I was able to get homeowners to snap out of it.

STORYTIME: WHAT HAPPENS IN VEGAS

There are elements of the Blandification that disturb me: the lack of color, the lack of effort, the lack of contrast—but the lack of personalization in homes is what really sticks in my craw about the Blandification trend. I first realized this in Las Vegas of all places when my husband and I took our first solo trip post-baby around 2007. We had an absolutely lovely experience at the Mandalay Bay hotel. I spent extra time in the hotel room thanks to food poisoning that I likely contracted from the Detroit airport cafeteria, so I had plenty of time to take note of subtle differences between the décor in the hotel room and the décor trends that I was witnessing in client homes.

Over dinner at Aerole as I watched the wine angels fly up two stories to fetch a highly-recommended bottle of bordeaux, I talked with my husband about the beige trend comparison. "Do you know what I discovered today during my food poisoning epiphany?" I asked him. He slowly set his wine glass down and replied "What happens in Vegas stays in Vegas?"

remodeling your house without killing your spouse

I snorted my wine and replied "No! I discovered that our hotel room has more character, interest and personality than any of my clients' homes. The problem isn't just the beige anymore. It's a fundamental stripping of all things personal from homes that's causing the Blandification." "Well, fix it." he helpfully replied. So I did.

My first goal in correcting the Blandification trend was to define what I meant by "personality" in home décor. Since I was raised in a home that was a good reflection of our family, I thought carefully about the tangible expressions that made our home a *home*. There are three elements I discovered were responsible for this feeling of belonging and personality. In order to achieve personality in your décor, your home should be a reflection of:

1. who you are
2. where you come from
3. what you believe in

My second goal was to get clients to realize what tangible items they owned that fell into this trio of reflection. I had a challenging time getting good results when I asked the question "What items do you have that are a direct reflection of who you are, where you come from and what you believe in?" Instead, I took inspiration one day while listening to 80's music and the Cinderella ballad "Don't Know What You Got (Till It's Gone)" popped up. I asked the question from a loss standpoint instead of a current inventory,

do:
fire test

and the results of reflection were amazing. Ready for an activity to demonstrate the importance of the reflection trio and measure how much personality your home actually has?

Fire Test

Imagine this scenario for me: your home is on fire. You have 90 seconds to retrieve and save those items which are sentimental and are NOT REPLACEABLE by insurance. Quickly now, your seconds are ticking. What will you save?

Having given this Fire Test hundreds of times over the years, I will help by explaining these rules:

1. Your family is safe. No worries. We're just talking about the irreplaceable sentimental stuff, so off you go.
2. Your pets are safe. Seriously, start thinking about those important keepsakes now. The fire is spreading.
3. Your important documents are safe. If your mind is going to those things, I'll start calling you Blandy McBlanderson now.
4. Your collection of eleventy billion 4x6 snapshots in a box under the bed doesn't count. If you appreciated them, you'd have them out for viewing (and should have them saved digitally anyway). Tick tock. Fire's raging.
5. No, you don't have superhuman strength. We're talking stuff hanging on the walls or easily grabbable. You're overthinking

remodeling your house without killing your spouse

this and the fire has consumed most everything now.

6. Guys, if you even think about listing your 52" LED flatscreen tv, I will fucking throat punch you. Seriously, IRREPLACEABLE is what I'm going for here.

Time's up. So what did you save from the fire?

The most common salvaged items from the Fire Test include things from these three categories:

1. Stuff from dead relatives (Grandpa's vintage camera collection, Grandma's quilt, Great Uncle Owen's medal from WWII).

2. Stuff your kids made (handprints, grade school drawings, a vase made in art class)

3. Generational pieces (antique dining chairs with Aunt Audrey's custom needlepoint seats that have been in the family for 100 years, Grandpa's high chair, letters home from the Civil War).

The expressions on the faces of the folks in the audience when I give this test during seminars is absolutely priceless. Some are horrified that there are SO many irreplaceable things on their list that 90 seconds isn't enough time to save them all, and others are stunned that they honestly couldn't give a shit if they lost everything today.

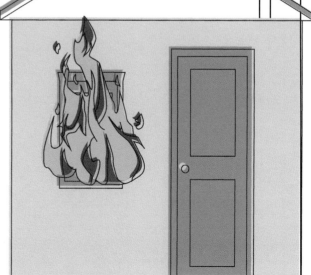

Here's the thing: if you could go out and re-purchase every single item in your home right now because none of it is personally meaningful to you, then there isn't enough shit you could ever buy to fill the hole in your soul. You, my friend, are living in a hotel room instead of a home. There are no roots to bind you or give you a personal connection to the space, and that just kills me.

The purpose of the Fire Test is to put into perspective how many of your possessions have meaning. If your list of salvaged items was long, then pat yourself on the back for being able to express through your décor who you are, where you come from and what you believe in. If your Fire Test list was short or blank, then we have some work to do.

If your list of salvage items was endless, you might have too much stuff. Think about your possessions with the same thought process as Christmas décor: you get it out for a few weeks a year, you think about the awesome memories, then gladly put it away knowing

If your fire test revealed items that you value but aren't currently on display, consider working them into your decor for the remodel.

you'll see it again. Consider doing this with too much everyday stuff: rotate your displays like a traveling museum to keep the focus on a few important items. Remember: too much repetition is NOT A THING.

The good news is that there are many awesomely easy, inexpensive and fun ways to add personality to your home. Let's take a look at a few categories of coolness to create some décor that would be salvage-worthy for your next Fire Test.

Peter WALSH

Peter Walsh, Professional Organizer, has helped many a hoarder overcome their issues with too much stuff. In one episode of Clean Sweep, Walsh encouraged a woman with a large collection of her deceased mother's items to reduce the display size so that she could better honor her mother's memory. The display was so overwhelming that she wasn't paying attention to any individual pieces within the collection, so thinning the herd would allow her to appreciate each piece.

What to Frame

Magazines: One of my prized possessions is a Popular Science magazine cover from 1966. I took a stack of magazines from my Dad's house after he passed away and I was immediately drawn to the November cover because of the fascinating articles listed, the great colors, and the address label in the bottom corner that was still intact bearing my Dad's name. I framed the cover with a colorful mat and it hangs proudly in my dining room.

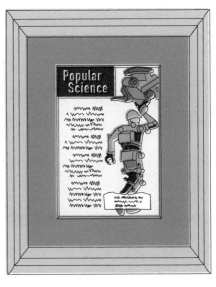

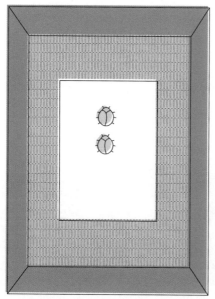

Greeting Card: I often have Fire Test takers mention stacks of greeting cards for their salvage list. If a card is that meaningful, think about displaying it permanently. I have a lovely card that a friend gave me on a trip to Hawaii. I framed it using a seagrass textured mat so I could recall the feeling of the beach. My vacation buddy died shortly after the trip, so I treasure it and think happy thoughts of our friendship each time I see the framed greeting card.

Documents: Handwriting pre-1950 is just cool. The loopy script is an art form that is slowly dying, so I love to frame pieces like personal letters, marriage certificates, diary pages, or anything else that allows a glimpse back in time. My 1870's Queen Anne Victorian home in upstate NY had telegrams from 1920-1930 thumb-tacked to the beams in the basement, so I mounted the original text messages in a floating frame so both sides were able to be viewed.

remodeling your house without killing your spouse

What to Create

Date Night Experience

Remember my food poisoning epiphany in Vegas? Once I recovered, the dining experience we had at Aerole was so amazing that I wanted to always remember it. As a huge foodie, I was giddy when the chef came out and autographed our menu. I got permission from the waiter to steal a napkin with the branding on it and tucked those items in my suitcase. When we returned home, I found a perfect size serving tray to hang flat on the wall and mount the menu with the napkin resting on the bottom. Every time I walk by it, I find myself humming "Bright light city gonna set my soul....gonna set my soul on fire."

Functional Recipes

Recipes also pop up frequently in the
Fire Test, so my favorite way to honor recipe cards instead
of hiding the tiny treasures in a book or box is to display
the ones that you reference most often and hang them in
your kitchen. No worries if the recipe cards are in rough
shape—the stains, spills and torn corners just show signs
of love. Think creatively about the display and break out
Grandma's wooden spoon. Mount the wooden spoon
horizontally on the wall, then use kitchen twine to hang
framed recipes from the spoon.   You can also mount the
recipes on old wooden cutting boards or vintage pie tins.

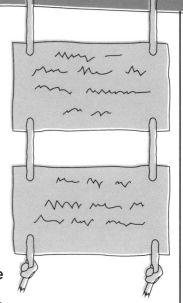

Travel Memories

I cringe every time I see cheesy photo frames with gimmicky back-
grounds showing a perfectly posed and tan family on vacation.
Sense memory is more powerful, so remember to capture and display the elements of the travel experience that made you
happy. Try using a vintage suitcase with the top removed to mount on the wall.   Your favorite picture
of the scenery or a sunset can be enlarged and used
as the backdrop for any other mementos—collections
of shells, an empty bottle of wine—the possibilities are
endless.

Wall of Cheese

I'd like to address the issue of photography for a hot minute. I've seen countless families dedicate entire hallways and stairways to their ever-changing progeny. One client in particular hired me to discuss rearranging her massive photo wall since another baby was on the way. As we stood and plotted the changes, her three year old son ran by on a constant loop around the room wearing

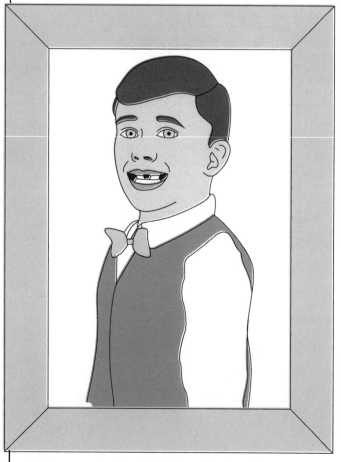

nothing but undies and a superman cape. He was adorable as his mom rooted for him to fly-fly-fly-fly by us each time. It was clear that she loved his antics and encouraged his creativity. When I looked back at the Olan Mills-style Wall of Cheese, I couldn't see the little superhero in any of the portraits. Instead, I saw a very proper preschooler with a forced grin and bored expression, but there was no evidence of the fabulous caped wonder in any of the frames. The realization made me sad, so I asked the mom this: "When your little Superman is grown,

do you want to look at these pictures and remember his physical appearance or the essence of his character?"
She was startled for a minute, then replied "Well.....I hadn't really thought about it."

I was more direct with the next question as I pointed to the Wall of Cheese. "Is this your son," I began, "or is THIS your son" I said, capturing superman as he flew by and tickling him until he squealed.

"Superman," she responded. I suggested that she completely rethink the Wall of Cheese, and I immediately put her in touch with a great photographer who specialized in candid shots of families. When the project was completed, she had a perfect picture of her little superman. This time, however, he was was caped, laughing, and his eyes were full of little-boy mischief. Some of the Wall of Cheese remains to appease the mother-in-law who bought the formal portrait sessions, but the candids sprinkled in do a much better job of telling the real story of who they are.

Character Hall of Fame

Harry POTTER Piece

One of my favorite clients commissioned me to create this art piece made of wood upcycled from a shipping pallet. When my client's three boys were younger, they read the entire Harry Potter series together as a family. She wanted the piece to hang in the living room with a quote from the series as a constant reminder of the family's character.

I used heavy cardstock and painstakingly cut out and placed every one of the letters, then decoupaged them with four coats of Mod Podge. The paint, distressing and hat details were added at the end.

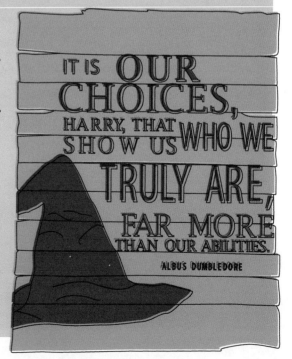

As a special surprise, I hid a few other favorite quotes in sharpie marker along the edges of the pallet. This piece of décor not only looks cool, but also perfectly reflects the values of my client's family.

IT IS OUR CHOICES, HARRY, THAT SHOW US WHO WE TRULY ARE, FAR MORE THAN OUR ABILITIES.

ALBUS DUMBLEDORE

Character Hall of Fame

Perfect PILLOW Piece

During a large remodel project, my client came to my studio with a paper grocery bag filled with jeans that had belonged to her two daughters. Sadly, the girls had been killed in a drunk driving accident a few years before. "I know you're creative, so do something with these," she said, handing me the denim treasures. "I trust you."

Knowing that it would be a sentimental accessory, I put my quilting skills to work and created a toss pillow for her new sofa. The quilt layout utilized pocket pieces from both of the daughters' jeans. While the client was thrilled with the outcome, the meaningful accessory had a more important impact: she took the pillow with her to therapy and hugged it tight to help her deal with the loss of her girls.

Over the last decade, I've witnessed and helped bring about a tremendous amount of change in the homes of many clients. My ultimate goals for those clients have always been centered around four core aspects of design:

1. helping them determine how they relate to both the space and each other in that space
2. understanding the importance of proper prioritizing and budgeting
3. helping them discover a new language of design to better communicate their wishes and needs to each other
4. creating décor that is an accurate reflection of who they are, where they come from, and what they believe in.

Being invited into someone's home for the express purpose of ripping it apart and putting it back together is a daunting task. I see the same look on the faces of clients halfway through the remodeling process as I recall seeing on my husband's face when our baby was two months old and crying constantly: "What. The fuck. Did. We get. Ourselves. Into?" This look is a marker of deep questioning of all that you felt you knew and all that you realize you don't know. The correlation between new parenting and the world of remodeling is remarkably similar in that way; couples end up questioning whether they should have tackled the project and if their relationship is actually strong enough to survive it.

I have seen enough of these "looks" between clients over the years to feel compelled to write about it. The sections of Communication, Cash, CRAP and Character are precisely the elements I use during a remodel project to avoid "the look" between clients. Educated clients are happy clients, so I began many years ago teaching couples the basic skills found in these chapters. When I found a formula that worked, I turned the info into a seminar so that even more folks could benefit. When enough folks from the audience asked me to write a book, I gladly complied.

 My hope for Remodeling Your House without Killing Your Spouse is that couples are able to experience a healthy, productive, painless remodel free from the threat of homicide and divorce. Working through the planning phases and properly using the worksheets as well as the BRAIN throughout the project is the best way I can prepare you to be successful (short of hiring me, which is an option as well. Just sayin').

If you would like to learn more about hiring HDD to help with your remodel either on-site or through e-consult, we'd love to hear from you through the Hart-Davidson Designs facebook page or the www.designisademocracy.com website. The HDD staff and I would be thrilled to help you live better in your home.

Need to access the forms listed in the book? Please visit the Remodeling Your House without Killing Your Spouse website at www.hddbook.com. You'll be able to check out bonus features including downloadable worksheets , funny behind-the-scenes pictures and stories, a glimpse of life in the HDD studio along with upcoming book signings and appearances. As more edutaining books are added to the HDD collection, they'll be promoted on the hddbook.com site as well.

 I sincerely wish you a happy, productive remodel free from homicide and divorce so that you and your spouse can live better in your home. Take care!

index

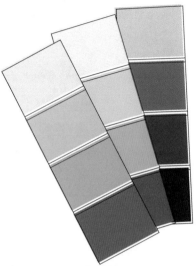

Leslie Hart-Davidson has helped thousands of people transform their houses into more livable, more lovable homes. She turned the interior design formula inside out in 2001 when she launched Hart-Davidson Designs (HDD) and began helping her clients understand the science behind the art of design.

Leslie's approach to interior design is as revolutionary to that industry as Apple's approach to computing and consumer electronics. And the two are similar. By focusing relentlessly on creating the best possible "experience" for clients - in their homes, offices, or wherever they may be - she delivers truly outstanding services and products. Design is not about making rooms beautiful, it's about making living and working beautiful.

But revolutionizing design practice is not easy. Disrupting the myth of the "genius designer," Leslie collaborates with her clients. How else can you transform lives and the experience of living and not just make pretty rooms?

The HDD tagline "Design is a Democracy, not a Dictatorship" sums up the revolutionary process that Leslie shares in this book. Whether it's teaching clients about the science of color and the wonders of human perception, or helping them learn a new design vocabulary to better communicate with their family members, what is routine for Leslie is 180 degrees from "standard" design practice. In the traditional design world, clients pay for the closely held secrets of a talented designer. The result: a designer's vision and another glossy room porn shot in the portfolio.

Leslie aims higher. She listens and works with clients to understand how transforming their space might lead to transforming their day-to-day activities, and over time, their lives for the better. And then she works tirelessly to set that transformation in motion.

With this, her first book, Leslie puts some of that transformative power into the hands of readers everywhere looking to live better in their homes. Vive la revolucion!

BHD